Can't Get No Satisfaction

A Quest for Racial Equality in Northern Florida in 1965

FRANKLIN REIDER

Tasora

COVER PHOTO: This photo clearly demonstrates the disdain with which the St. Augustine authorities treated Dr. King during the civil rights clashes in 1964. Here Dr. King was placed in the back seat of a police car with a German Shepard and no police vigilance. We see him speaking calmly with Andrew Young while waiting to testify before a grand jury dealing with his attempt to enter a local segregated restaurant. Photo Shutterstock

Tasora

ISBN 978-1-948192-00-2

Tasora Books
5120 Cedar Lake Road
Minneapolis, MN 55416
(952) 345-4488
Distributed by Itasca Books

Printed in the U.S.A.

Table of Contents

FOREWORD

"You've got to be taught
Before it's too late
Before you are 6 or 7 or 8
To hate all the people
Your relatives hate
You've got to be carefully taught"

You've Got To Be Carefully Taught

By Richard Rodgers and Oscar Hammerstein
from *South Pacific*

INTRODUCTION

The "rape" case in Marianna and the "hanging" suicide in St. Augustine were two examples of the shock that I had facing racism in northern Florida during the summer of 1965.

Working as a civil rights legal intern was truly a labor of love. I was born into a privileged family and I felt I had an obligation to help people less blessed than I. It was a summer filled with meaningful events for me and eye-opening clashes with a civilization I had not known existed in my country of birth.

I decided to write this memoir, in great part, so that my five children and 10 grandchildren would have some insight into their heritage and the great significance that volunteering could have in their lives. It also describes an important historical time for our country in a very personal manner that could be educational for those young people that might happen upon this book.

In many respects we have come a long way toward equality for all races since 1965. Unfortunately, too many aspects of our life remain the same. While there has been unquestionable progress in achieving better opportunities for black citizens in the United States today, there still remains much to be done.

The justice system still comes down harder on people of color than on the white population and continued de facto segregation persists throughout most of the country. Predominantly black residential areas and predominantly black schools still do not receive their fair share of tax expenditures, although it has greatly improved in comparison to 50 years ago.

Police brutality toward people of color is an unfortunate fact of life across the country; yet in comparison to what it once was, huge progress has been made.

I hope this book can shed some light on what used to be to help understand what exists today. So many people of my generation helped make tiny steps toward equality in the face of the brutal repression of a power structure desirous to maintain a very unjust society.

The economic development in 19th century United States, principally in the South, was achieved through slavery and the exploitation of its black citizens. The maintenance of the slaves as poor and ignorant was fundamental to keeping the society stable and the economy flourishing.

Creating the myth that blacks are a sub-human, inherently ignorant, race, was essential for the otherwise religious people of the South to justify their exploitation of their black slaves.

When blacks began to achieve positions of importance after the Civil War, aided by progressive civil rights legislation and constitutional amendments, racist violence and ill-advised Supreme Court decisions destroyed this progress and re-established racist control of the southern states and, thereby, the suppression of black people's rights. The 20th century, in adapting to laws outlawing slavery, did not see fundamental change until the 1960s. And said change only came with the shedding of so much blood of very brave people.

I participated in many interesting cases while working for Mr. John Due, Esquire, in 1965. I cite two of the most memorable, those of Mariana and St. Augustine, both in Florida, because they clearly demonstrate what challenges existed at that time and how society and law functioned in regard to civil rights and the resistance to change.

The Marianna case offers a slice of life in racist times and, unfortunately, shows how unfairly blacks were treated as a matter of course. The St. Augustine chapter goes into much greater depth and follows a history of an important town where racism and discrimination were a fact of life and the local government resisted any change, even when its economy was being crushed. The nation watched in horror as the lowest level of local townspeople smashed any and all attempts to achieve equality for its black population, while the state and local leadership silently resisted the social change that was beginning to happen elsewhere in the country.

It is hard to fully grasp the enormous courage of the people that participated in the civil rights movement for those who only know about it through history books. The people who braved violence in order to register blacks to vote all over the South were true heroes as much as the soldiers who fought in the world wars to protect our country.

This book would not have been completed without the support and nudging of my son, Dylan, my daughter, Vanessa, and my wife, Vera. I am grateful for how they have helped me. That said, any mistakes herein are all mine.

I also want to thank my tireless editor, Carol Csomay, as well as David Nolan, Regina Gayle Phillips, and Gwendolyn Duncan, all from St. Augustine, for their orientation about their town today and historically. A special thanks goes out to my granddaughter, Devin Goldman who made crucial suggestions and Marcelo Guanabara, who took fabulous photographs of important locations in St. Augustine.

CHAPTER ONE

MY BACKGROUND

In the beginning of my freshman year in high school I happily greeted a black student that I had become friendly with over the years through baseball. He pushed me away and told me to never talk to him again. I was shocked.

During lunch break, I went into the boys' room and shortly thereafter a group of six black kids came in and surrounded me. Anthony, the black kid who pushed me away, came up to me and challenged me to a fight. His friends were screaming at him to get it on. I told him I had no reason to fight him and was not going to. He told me I had to fight or he was going to beat me up. I made an attempt to reason with him, while his friends screamed crazily for blood in the background. Suddenly he turned and told them to shut up.

"You gotta fight me, man!" he yelled at me as he raised his fists.

My hands were down by my side and I repeated I was not going to do that. "We were always friends on the team," I said. "I do not know what happened to you over the summer but I have not changed. If you no longer are friends with me, that is your choice. But I have no reason to fight you, so I won't."

Anthony dropped his fists in frustration. "Let him out," he said loudly to his friends. "Just let him out."

I left the boys' room and there were no further incidents with Anthony, although he no longer played baseball on the school team and we had virtually no further contact until we both graduated high school together. We met at a reunion celebrating 50 years since our graduation and I asked him if he remembered that interaction. He laughed and said he had no recollection.

My family had moved to Westbury, Long Island, New York when I was nine years old. I went through the public school system, graduating from high school in 1960. The student population was very mixed, predominantly white, with a large immigrant influence.

Approximately 20% of our high school was black, with an equal number of first-generation Italian. My contact with the black students was mostly through sports. I played varsity basketball, tennis and baseball and made friends with a few black athletes.

My relations with other students was quite varied for those times but socially the groups were mostly self-segregated. I had another very tense racial incident in high school.

The second incident happened in the beginning of basketball season in my sophomore year. I was the co-captain of the junior varsity team and we were having a pre-season game against our varsity. It should have been totally one-sided in their favor but we were playing well and I was having a day where everything I threw up went in.

At halftime I had over 20 points and the game was very close. I was a very skinny kid with a terrific outside shot and there were a few special days where it seemed like I could not miss. This was one such day.

As we warmed up for the second half, a big, black classmate of mine who was a starter on the varsity team came over to us and shouted at me. Using multiple curse words, he warned me not to make any more shots during the second half.

His warning included a threat. If I were to make any more baskets he was going to get me in the shower after the game and stick his member into my mouth. As he was a big kid, a bully, this was not a threat to take lightly. However, I remained focused on the game.

As the second half began the ball came to me and I drove to the basket and made a layup around the defense of the very player who had threatened me minutes earlier. He screamed at me that he would get me after the game and by then everyone on both teams knew what was going to happen. I continued to play my game and scored well although we lost as the varsity came on strong at the end.

Everyone on both teams walked to the locker room with great apprehension. I had no idea what I was going to do but I was not going to run away and I was not going to ask the coaches for help.

Before I could take off my uniform, one of the reserve players on the varsity came up to me and told me to sit where I was. He then went up to the black player and told him to leave me alone and if he did not like it, to meet him outside the school and settle up there. So the showers were fortunately uneventful.

As I was leaving the locker room, the student who saved me told me to go home, to not come see the fight. I found out later that he destroyed the black student in the fight. Unfortunately, the black student got in trouble during the following summer and dropped out of school. Two years later, in what would have been his senior year, he was shot and killed in an attempted robbery. I feel indebted to the student, Roger Silver, who saved me that day. I remember all the details as vividly as if it happened yesterday.

The '60s were one of the most exciting decade of my life. I graduated high school, poorly read and politically unaware. I headed off to Carleton College in Northfield Minnesota, super knowledgeable about all things sports. My closet at home was filled with shoe boxes of baseball cards.

My father had taught me that all people were equal and everyone deserved respect. However, in my insular upbringing, I never had to put such thinking into practice.

Carleton was at the time, and still is, considered to be one of the top small schools in the country. Life magazine had a multi-page article on it in the spring of 1960, with the headline "The Harvard of the Midwest."

The student body consisted of very successful students with high intellectual abilities and interests. Debates raged on campus about Fidel Castro and Cuba. Carleton had a very outspoken group demanding fair play for Cuba.

At that time I knew nothing about the issues involved. For reasons I never understood, I was elected to the college senate my freshman year. There were two senators from each class and as a result of the student activism on campus, the positions the senate took on issues important to the student body became crucial.

Interestingly, the dean of students was very conservative and made his disagreements with the liberal student body quite vocal. When he learned that I was a new senator, he seemed to bump into me multiple times and asked me questions about issues of which I knew nothing. The need to learn about this and other matters, including those related to race relations, became paramount for me.

It seemed like every night, people would gather in my room to discuss politics. I quickly became aware of the issues involved and did a lot of reading and research.

I discovered that newspapers had sections besides sports. The library had newspapers from around the world and I made it a habit before studying to read a few almost daily. This began an awakening for me about the social issues of the day and gradually I became knowledgeable and very much involved. I tended toward the more liberal positions and the issue of race became quite important to me.

In my sophomore and junior years, I had friends who went south during the summer to Mississippi to work for voter registration drives. I was fascinated with the civil rights movement and felt unequivocally that racial discrimination was not only wrong but also an embarrassment to our country, which, we were taught, was the fairest system in the world.

I felt strongly that the federal government had to get more involved to force integration and to protect blacks who wanted to vote and attend public schools in the South.

One of the myths I was taught in high school was the idea that the Civil War was fought over states' rights. Any real student of history knows the unquestionable truth is that the Civil War was fought over slavery. After the North won, Congress passed numerous laws outlawing the separation of races and requiring equal access to facilities, government and otherwise.

But when Andrew Johnson, a poor Tennessean, became president after Lincoln's assasination, he helped the South avoid having to obey these new laws and return to their segregationist ways. Part and parcel with these efforts was the promulgation of the myth that states' rights was at the core of the war. That this myth took hold in our country to the point that history classes even in the North taught this is something that rankles me even today.

But returning to my budding interest in social issues, Fidel Castro had become a folk hero and I felt President Kennedy was a bully in regard to Cuba. Castro's experiment with communist rule was untested at the time and the economic embargo that the U.S. put on Cuba seemed unfair to me, especially in view of the fact that JFK openly smoked Cuban cigars, the use of which was illegal in our country.

By 1963 the presence of American "advisors" in the Far East had become a big issue on campus and I felt it was a serious mistake. By the time I graduated in 1964, I felt our most important issue was to get out of Vietnam and, secondly, to remove the ban on Cuba. At that time I was in the minority on both issues. Racial inequality and its accompanying discrimination was a subject of constant concern, especially as the civil rights movement began to grab headlines and racial clashes were reported nightly on the news.

Before I entered law school in the fall of 1964, two Jewish kids from Brooklyn were murdered along with a local black kid in a small town in Mississippi. This shocked me tremendously.

I had been a camp counselor in the Pocono Mountains of Pennsylvania, far removed from the goings on of the real world. I decided that this would be my last year at camp where I had gone every summer but one since I was nine years old. I felt strongly I had to somehow get involved to change the discrimination against blacks in our country.

CHAPTER TWO

LAW STUDENTS CIVIL RIGHTS RESEARCH COUNCIL

In June, 1965,I took my first Greyhound bus ride from Atlanta to Tallahassee. I was not prepared for the shock that the south presented. At our first stop, I was confronted by separate bathrooms, one for "Whites" and one for "Coloreds." I used the colored bathroom.

When I exited it, there were a few white gentlemen outside apparently unhappy with my choice. I looked at them and, as I walked to the bus, they mumbled some disparaging words as I passed by and boarded. This was my first upfront meeting with segregation.

It would not take long to learn that in a segregated society so many actions we take, no matter how mundane the act, such as going to the bathroom, becomes a political action. "Which side are you on boy, which side are you on?"

I was to begin a summer internship working in northern Florida for a civil rights lawyer when the above incident occurred.

In 1963, students from a few Ivy League law schools created an organization to help lawyers working on cases related to civil rights. The concept was to offer talented students, at no cost to the attorneys, who could help do research for cases that frequently generated little or no income, but were important to advance the cause of civil rights.

In the summer of 1963, a small number of these students worked for lawyers in a variety of cities in the northern United States. Shortly after its creation, the students were able to get the Law Students Civil Rights Council (LSCRC) registered as a charity whose contributions paid for the legal interns' maintenance while in these jobs.

In 1964, the LSCRC raised enough money to allow a greater number of students to take these intern jobs. Although the number was still modest, they made a serious contribution to the development of a number of important cases.

By the end of 1964, a multitude of organizations had contributed significant funds, which permitted approximately 100 spaces to be funded for the following summer, with multiple locations around the country, this time including a number of the southern states as well.

According to *TIME* magazine, (May 21,1965) 342 students applied for summer intern positions, with 177 being offered positions, 97 rejected and 68 put on the waiting list.

I entered NYU School of Law in September 1964 but only heard about LSCRC in the spring of 1965. I immediately applied to go south, but was told that all of the positions had been filled. When I spoke with my parents, my father generously offered to fund any costs that would be involved if I could get an assignment.

It was not an easy decision for them, as two student volunteers from Brooklyn were murdered in Mississippi in June of 1964 for attempting to register blacks to vote. The repercussions of these murders, along with that of a local black student there, had heavy publicity all over the country and most especially in the New York area.

Events like these had a seriously chilling effect on students intending to go south. But when my parents saw my determination to make a difference in the fight for civil rights, they supported my efforts.

As the end of the second semester of my freshman year of law school approached I was assigned to a lawyer in Tallahassee, Florida. We were to meet in early June in Atlanta, where we would be given transportation to Tallahassee after attending an orientation program.

Most of my friends and relatives tried to convince me not to go as they viewed this adventure as being extremely dangerous. Andrew Schwerner and Michael Goodman, the white Jewish Brooklynites who had been murdered in Mississippi, had become household names and symbols of the dangers that awaited any of us students trying to change the insidious institutions in the segregated South.

I, however, simply felt it was something I had to do and, stubbornly, did not feel moved by these cautionary entreaties of the people closest to me at this point in my life.

The orientation program in Atlanta was extremely well organized for the few dozen of us embarking on the program in this part of the country. We were taught that our concentration was on legal tasks, not other activities that involved marching, registering voters or other very public activities. We were not prohibited from participating but what was needed was heavy legal work. We were advised of the dangers of being viewed as northern agitators.

Discussing the deaths of Schwerner and Goodman was unavoidable. Integrated groups were not looked upon kindly by people dedicated to maintaining a segregated society. This phrase "not looked upon kindly" would be something I would hear repeatedly on a daily basis from people on all sides of the issue of integration during my time in the South. Also, virtually everyone I would meet would call me "son,"regardless of whether they were friend or foe.

Before we left for our assigned locations we had some special guests: Rev. Martin Luther King spoke to us about the importance of the legal process in the fight for civil rights. He emphasized that although the courts move slowly, they almost always end up doing the right thing. It was his conviction that in the end, it is our just legal system that is the bedrock of democracy and all of the lawyers on our side were crucial to eventually achieving equality.

Dr. King had an ethereal quality about him. When we shook his hand and he thanked us one by one, I felt he represented an almost godlike presence. He confronted challenges, criticism from allies and enemies alike, with grace and patience.

At this time, he was probably more hated than liked. Not only did the segregationists hate him for his efforts to "change their society," but many black leaders thought he was trying to go too fast. People from all over accused him of being a communist for fighting for equal access to fair- paying jobs.

CORE and SNCC members said he was going too slowly. At this time, CORE and SNCC were two civil rights organizations that mostly made of of younger members and wanted change quickly. In the next chapter I will detail each of these organizations and their importance. Some black leaders, especially those from SNCC, were critical of his philosophy of non-violence. They argued that it portrayed blacks as weak and played into the hands of the racists.

With all of this pulling and tugging, Dr. King stayed the course, his course. He was not perfect; he made mistakes. But his courage and determination are what led to new legislation and new inroads towards equality until meaningful changes eventually took place in our society.

CHAPTER THREE

NAACP, ET AL

The initials, NAACP, stand for National Association for the Advancement of Colored People. It was founded in 1909 to fight for "the betterment of colored people," according to its founder, the sociologist, W.E.B. Du Bois. Dr. Du Bois, as he liked to be called, wanted to move away from the Booker T. Washington approach of appeasement to advance the colored people in the world of segregated white society.

Although he wanted equality during his lifetime, the NAACP fought for better conditions for the black people but effectively put equality on a secondary plane. Its name said advancement and that is what its members effectively strove for. Equality was far off but advancement could be attained in small steps.

By the 1960s, the NAACP had become a conservative wing of the civil rights movement. The Southern Christian Leadership Conference (SCLC) was founded in 1957 and was led by Dr. Martin Luther King, Jr. until his assassination in 1968.

Spurred by the bus boycott in Montgomery, Alabama, the SCLC had as its expressed purpose to end segregation and achieve equality for all Negroes in the United States. Unlike the NAACP and CORE (Congress for Racial Equality), the SCLC established affiliates throughout the South primarily through black churches. The other organizations created offices using local leaders.

With Dr. King at the forefront, and using exclusively non-violent tactics, the civil rights movement was begun. However, it was very slow at first as segregationist organizations used very repressive tactics, whether through strong-armed police repression or the more violent acts of individual racists and the Ku Klux Klan (KKK).

Churches were hesitant to join as the local tendencies toward violence scared the local pastors and their congregations. But SCLC-led boycotts, sit-ins and marches garnered national attention and the violence that ensued stimulated people from other areas of the country to participate in the protests. College students went south during their vacation summers to help register voters, teach in black schools and demonstrate in local towns.

The NAACP, led by Roy Wilkins, and CORE, led by James Farmer, were crucial organizations in the civil rights movement. Wilkins was an outstanding speaker and had strong political ties within the Democratic Party. As he was known to be more conservative, he was able to keep open communications with politicians who felt Dr. King was trying to move too fast.

James Farmer was a fabulous speaker and a brave demonstrator as the leader of CORE. He was usually side by side at the demonstrations with Dr. King and his lieutenants.

In 1960, the Student Nonviolent Coordinating Committee (SNCC) was founded as the fourth important civil rights organization. One of its founders, Julian Bond, became its face.

A brilliant leader, Bond was also an excellent speaker and a brave voice in the civil rights movement. He was young, outspoken and sometimes brash. SNCC was viewed as the most aggressive and most left wing of the four organizations. Students flocked to it. Shortly thereafter, John Lewis, already well known for his courage and groundbreaking efforts to register voters and integrate public facilities and interstate buses became SNCC's leader.

In 1966, Stokely Carmichael was elected president of SNCC after being an active organizer in Alabama. Although initially a close ally of Dr. King and an active non-violent organizer, he and many other demonstrators tired of being beaten by white racist thugs.

Shortly after Carmichael became SNCC's leader, James Meredith, who was the first black to enter the University of Mississippi, was shot while marching in Mississippi. Meredith's admission had required the intervention of the federal government. There were incidents of violence and were even two murders of his supporters. Hence, his presence at the university required around-the-clock protection and unending controversy.

Carmichael quickly joined the demonstration and made a seminal speech denouncing non-violence and declaring that instead of marching for freedom he would be leading the cause for "Black Power."

Raising a fist, he became the symbol for change. He supported the Black Panthers, viewed, mistakenly in my opinion, as a violent group. He also renounced being called Negro and insisted on being either black or Afro-American. This speech led to the word Negro ultimately being cancelled as an acceptable description for a black person. It also precipitated multiple demonstrations of black power in numerous public settings, including the 1968 Olympics and the Democratic National Convention in Chicago in that same year.

After this split, Carmichael became separated from Dr. King both physically and philosophically. Dr. King called "Black Power" an "unfortunate choice of words." As a member of the Black Panthers, Carmichael looked upon non-violence as a "white" invention that effectively helped keep black people subjugated to the white "rulers."

His speech became more political and more radical. He visited communist leaders in North Vietnam and Cuba. Eventually he totally left the movement, moved to Africa and changed his name to Kwame Ture.

Dr. King never accepted calling Negroes blacks. However, following Carmichael's fiery speeches the language changed and, after Dr. King's assassination, the language and the movement changed as well.

One of the most important organizations in the civil rights movement was part of the NAACP. The Legal Defense Fund (LDF) was active early on in taking cases for black people who were discriminated against or in any way had their civil rights denied.

Its most famous lawyer was Thurgood Marshall, who began taking cases in the 1950s for the LDF and eventually became its lead counsel. The most significant achievement of both the LDF and Marshall was leading the legal team that won Brown v. Board of Education in 1954.

The Legal Defense Fund continues to be a force for equal rights until today and was crucial throughout the '60s in a step-by-step progression toward equal rights under the law. Marshall was appointed to the Supreme Court by President Lyndon Johnson, becoming its first black justice.

When I went south to work for John Due, Esq. in Tallahassee I had no real preference for any of the organizations. I was surprised, however, to see that CORE was a sponsor of John Due, with support from SNCC as well.

To my knowledge neither of these organizations were known to finance lawyers. Normally, financial support for civil rights lawyers came from associations with organizations created to offer legal support.

Mr. Due, unbeknownst to me, was only 31 in 1965. He had a much older, perhaps more mature, air to him and at my 22 years of age there seemed to me to be a wider age gap between us. His wife, Patricia Due, was a civil rights leader on her own. She led numerous demonstrations in the early '60s and was a very charismatic lady. She divided her time between Tallahassee and Miami where she was pursuing a degree at what is now known as Miami Dade College.

Most of my time in Tallahassee was spent working on cases for John Due. Many times it involved travel to other cities. Sometimes it involved legal research. But I became active with my fellow intern, Ira Simmons, in local affairs, mostly with students.

I joined my first demonstration with Ira and that led to participating in many tens of demonstrations all over northern Florida. I marched frequently with James Farmer, the head of CORE. We became friendly and I heard him speak many times.

He was a de facto second-in-command to Dr. King. Dr. King had his excellent lieutenants like Ralph Abernathy and Hosea Williams, but Farmer was a compatriot who spoke frequently at rallies, including the March On Washington in 1963, that were headlined by Dr. King.

Later these marches would cause me to cross paths with many other important figures in the civil rights movement. The Freedom Singers were initially a group of black demonstrators who began singing "We Shall Overcome" at marches around the South. They were members of SNCC. With no fame, they were just focused on civil rights.

I remember a demonstration in Mississippi in 1965 that was very tense. There were crowds of rowdy whites with sticks threatening the demonstrators. Police had been called but it was not clear whose side they would be on in the case of violence.

The Freedom Singers led our group. I cannot describe the feeling of singing "We Shall Overcome" under these circumstances. It made us all very brave and more determined to face the threat of violence. This repeated itself multiple times and it was inspiring to be with them. Later we caught up to each other at conferences and demonstrations in New York and Washington, D.C. They were very special people. When their album came out, *WE SHALL OVERCOME,* I happily bought it.

I had a split role in regard to demonstrations. Sometimes my role was as a legal adviser. This frequently entailed taking pictures of threatening white men and writing down license plate numbers. Often I was the only white person with the black demonstrators. Both the police and the potential attackers often would think I was the leader of the group, which was, in fact, never the case.

Other times, I was just another demonstrator who joined in because I believed in what was the cause of the demonstration. Frequently, I was a member of a small group trying to integrate a segregated restaurant. I was always an adherent to the philosophy of non-violence.

Although there were numerous close calls, I never suffered any actual violence. As I will relate, there were a series of incidents in St. Augustine that could have been seriously violent but were fortunately terminated before violence broke out.

All of these organizations played significant roles in the civil rights movement and all had their presence marked by charismatic, intelligent leadership. John Lewis, who was one of the bravest and smartest leaders of the '60s went on to become an important congressman from Atlanta. Andrew Young, one of Dr. King's important assistants, was a U.S. congressman, resigning to become ambassador to the United Nations, and, subsequently, mayor of Atlanta.

James Farmer became a professor at Mary Washington College, the women's college of the University of Virginia (UVA). Jesse Jackson, also a young assistant to Dr. King, became a national leader against the war in Vietnam and a candidate for U.S. president. Stokely Carmichael was an important national leader until he decided to move to Africa. Julian Bond was a significant leader, who served for 20 years as a Georgia legislator, chairman of the NAACP for 12 years and the first president of the Southern Poverty Law center. He also was a professor at many colleges, including Harvard and the University of Virginia (for 22 years), among others.

In my opinion, all of the above leaders, and many others, are American heroes whose bravery and vision should be celebrated. Although present day society still has racial divides, de facto segregation and numerous very serious issues in regard to race, the progress that has been achieved is dramatic and important for our society. There should be, in my opinion, more celebration of the efforts that these leaders have made in achieving the dramatic changes that have taken place in our country.

CHAPTER FOUR

SEPARATE BUT EQUAL

"Separate but Equal" is a concept created by southern white governments to keep blacks from socially mixing with whites. The thinking here is that "Negroes would prefer to be with their own just like us whites prefer to be with our own."

So if a city, county or state offered public access to a school or a bathroom in a bus station or any other of a multitude of facilities, in order to protect the purity of the white race, the same facility would be offered to "Negroes" and each race would only use the facility created for them. Signs that said "Whites Only" or "Colored" to identify which were which were the norm all over the South.

The Supreme Court of the United States had played a crucial role in furthering the legalization of Negro inferiority and, by extension, white supremacy in many ill-conceived decisions.

In 1857, the Dred Scott decision held that the Negro race was inferior and therefore the members of their race were not citizens of the country. This served as the basis for the concept of white supremacy in the courts and in general life.

Subsequently, the court held various post-Civil War equal-rights legislation unconstitutional.

In 1896, the United States Supreme Court upheld the constitutionality of Separate but Equal in Plessy v. Ferguson for public facilities. The decision was a 7-1 vote, with the lone dissent written by Justice John Marshall Harlan.

This was a landmark decision. What is not so well known is that what brought the case to the Supreme Court was the conflict between the southern states' laws promulgating separate facilities and the federal laws passed after the Civil War requiring all public facilities to be integrated.

The aforementioned decisions used the concept of "states' rights" to allow discriminatory local practices to be legal.

Justice Harlan came from a prominent Kentucky family, which owned slaves, and was previously an attorney general of Kentucky who defended slavery. Later in life and before being appointed to the Supreme Court, he changed his views on slavery and segregation and became an advocate for equality for blacks.

Curiously, his landmark dissent, frequently quoted as a vision for equality, specifically excluded other races from his opinion, most particularly people of Chinese origin. He stated in this dissent that Chinese people should be excluded from entering the U.S. and should not be protected under the Constitution!

One of the many harmful effects of the Plessy decision was the emboldening of segregationists to expand discriminatory policies in all walks of life throughout the South. Before Plessy, blacks participated in the electoral process in many of the southern states.

For instance, Louisiana had many thousands of black voters and even black legislators. Both North and South Carolina had black congressmen and a black senator. Beginning after Plessy, the southern states started to pass laws to disenfranchise blacks. It became arduous to register to vote and for those already registered, to maintain their voting status. By early in the 20th century, the number of blacks registered to vote was reduced radically. In 1896, Louisiana had 130,334 black registered voters. In 1904, there were only 1,342.

Mississippi passed laws after Plessy to disenfranchise previously registered black voters and by 1901 the process was complete.

The ramifications of these decisions were felt in the social fiber of the South as white violence against black became rampant, most especially where there had been social advancement for blacks after the passing of post-Civil War civil rights legislation.

Upcoming chapters will discuss the effects of white violence against blacks right up to and through the 1960s.

In 1954, the concept of Separate but Equal was held unconstitutional by the Supreme Court in Brown v. The Board of Education. The vote was 9-0. This implied that all public facilities had to be integrated and all races had to have equal access. To say the least, the implementation of this ruling in the South was very slow in coming. The Florida State Legislature passed a bill stating the Brown decision was invalid in its state. The civil rights movement was all about making the Brown ruling a reality.

For a middle-class white boy raised in Westbury, Long Island in a Jewish family that believed in equality for all, the concept of separation of races and all aspects of racism was abhorrent.

I arrived in Tallahassee, Florida by bus having travelled from Atlanta, Georgia where my orientation was given. Each bus stop was a shock. The bathrooms were separate and the signs were clear: Every time I urinated I was taking a stand in favor or against segregation!

When I would use the "colored" bathroom, there frequently were unhappy faces and threats from whites when I exited. For me, it was the first of many uncomfortable instances of reality in a segregated world.

The Plessy decision emphasized that to be legal, the facilities had to be equal. The defense by segregationists was that since they were equal there was really nothing that was objectionable.

Setting aside the argument that the concept was inherently unfair, the fact is that the facilities were almost never equal. White janitors would not clean "colored" bathrooms so the facilities in a bus station were revolting in the "colored" bathrooms. This helped perpetuate the myth that blacks were sloppy, lazy, dirty, etc. The fact is that the white bathroom was cleaned up regularly and the "colored" rarely.

Shortly after arriving in Tallahassee, my fellow intern, Ira Simmons, took me around the city. We visited Florida State University (FSU), the largest public university in the state. It was magnificent. The campus was dominated by beautiful trees and bright green grass. All were neatly cut and well maintained.

The colonial architecture with large white columns was the norm for the buildings. Fraternity Row was out of a movie. I had visited friends at Ohio State while in college and was overwhelmed by its magnificence. Florida State was even more impressive.

Then Ira took me to Florida A&M (Florida Agricultural and Mechanical University), a predominantly black school, where he had graduated college. The contrast was shocking. The roads were dirt, whereas the ones throughout FSU were paved and neatly kept. The trees at A&M were mostly palms that were poorly maintained. The buildings seemed to be Army issued, as if on a military base. Equal was not an adjective that would describe Florida A&M.

The budgets allocated by the state legislature were majorly different, with A&M getting a fraction of what was destined for FSU. The salaries of the professors at each school obviously reflected this disparity. Once again, equal was not a part of the life in segregated Florida.

The common belief in Tallahassee in 1965 was that FSU was totally segregated, that no race other than white attended the school. However, in fact, there was a black student in the undergraduate school. ONE! There were also a few in the graduate schools. Reportedly there were three in the '60s.

However, they went to class and then home. They did not socialize or become members of clubs on campus. They were not on sports teams nor did they eat in the student union. They were pawns in the segregationist pattern. This concept was "Tokenism."

Instead of standing up to the law, as Governor George Wallace did in Alabama, many states like Florida would allow a token black into the schools and other institutions to avoid public attention and public criticism. But the segregation was fundamentally unchanged. As was the case of FSU, most times it even went unnoticed.

To illustrate this phenomenon, Ira and I had a very interesting happening. One night during my dive into the realities of the South, Ira told me that there had never been a black person that had eaten at the FSU student union.

The student union for most colleges and universities is the social center for students. In between classes they could get a soda or a sandwich, chat with friends or study for their next class. It was a fundamental part of the student experience. Visitors would almost always stop by to get a feel of the campus. Frequently, eating a snack or buying a tee shirt was part of the visit. That it was forbidden for non-whites to go there seemed to me to be incongruous to what the university should be about.

"Get used to that, Frank," Ira remarked with a smirk. "This is the South"

We discussed other similar types of discrimination. Finally, I asked him if he wanted to do something about it. He was vehement in his reaction.

"When? Let's do it!"

Over the next few days we discussed how we would go about it. One night Ira told me his girlfriend wanted to join us. As for so many black students, she was fed up with discrimination in all parts of life in Florida.

The status quo was unacceptable and she wanted to be in the forefront of this change. Furthermore, as a student at A&M, she was aware that FSU was the school of privilege. While most students were proud of A&M, they knew it would be much improved with a fair share of state funding.

I told Ira that, for me, she was more than welcome to join us. I had never participated in the integrating of a previously segregated facility. The only step in that direction that I had taken up to then was using the "colored" bathrooms in gas stations and bus stops. Little did I know that this would be my first attempt in a long series of such acts.

We decided that the next Saturday would be the day. It was sort of a day off for us and probably the student union would be less crowded.

"Does your girlfriend have a friend?" I asked half seriously.

"She does, and she is gorgeous. And I am sure she feels the same way. I will see."

That was the plan and on Saturday Ira and the two ladies picked me up to go have lunch at FSU. Ira had a convertible and he had the top down. A mixed couple in 1965 Tallahassee was intolerable to segregationists and could invite trouble in and of itself. In a convertible driving onto the FSU campus would be virtually unheard of. But that is exactly what we did.

We arrived in the parking lot and walked to the student union. Climbing up the steps immediately caused comments from the few students who were around. Ira and I were in jeans. The women were dressed up and very presentable.

We found what turned out to be a student restaurant with waitresses, not a place where you ordered and took your food to a table. We sat down at a place for four and shortly thereafter a waitress came to our table. We all ordered hamburgers and Cokes.

Slowly, groups of students gathered and watched us. As time passed, bigger male students pushed to the front of the groups. There were loud rumblings but no direct shouts toward us yet.

Ira was the most experienced at these sorts of events and he said that we had to be aware of what is going on and be ready to leave. Our area was oval in shape and had only one entrance/exit. As our order arrived at the table, the observers became more rowdy.

"This is not a place for niggers," shouted one.

"You bastards better get out of here while you can," shouted another.

I looked to Ira for guidance. The women were silent but determined to stay if Ira wanted to do so.

The shouting grew. We kind of lost our respective appetites.

Ira spoke. "I think we should leave now".

"OK," I responded. "You all go first and get in the car. I will pay the bill and meet you downstairs. If it gets too dangerous to wait for me, you leave and I will walk home."

They got up and left. So far as I could see no one harmed them as they exited. The waitress rapidly gave me the bill and I paid her, adding a generous tip. "Sorry we could not stay longer," I said, smiling.

She nodded without returning my smile and walked away.

I headed for the exit. Some of the biggest guys I had ever seen were blocking the way.

"Why are you here?" a huge blond gentleman asked me.

I reminded myself that my New York sense of sarcasm would not be welcome here. I politely responded.

"I had never been to the FSU campus and wanted to get a hamburger and see everything."

"Yeah. OK, but not with niggers. Niggers can't come here."

I did not respond to his racism. "Excuse me," I said as I moved around him.

He opened a path for me but cautioned. "Don't come back here with any niggers. You will regret it if you do."

They followed me down the stairs. Ira was waiting. I literally jumped into the car and we took off.

Neither back then nor today am I sure if we had a victory at FSU.

However it was clear that Separate but Equal did not apply to the Florida university system in 1965. Except for the Separate part. That dominated.

CHAPTER FIVE

TOKENISM

After 'Separate But Equal' was held unconstitutional in 1954, efforts were made by the civil rights movement to integrate schools, register black voters, eat in previously all-white public facilities, and, in general, make segregation a part of the past. The changes were very slow in coming and by the 1960s reports of clashes became commonplace in the newspapers and on TV.

Local governments all over the South had to face the movement and there were a variety of ways governors, mayors and sheriffs dealt with these social issues. Governors like George Wallace of Alabama and Lester Maddox of Georgia made supporting segregation their mantra.

The federal government had to be called into action to force desegregation of the schools. Clashes broke out all over the South and many local sheriffs became symbols of resistance to integration.

Both Selma and Montgomery, Alabama were scenes of horrible violence imposed by police, with blacks being trampled by horse-riding police. Water hoses with maximum force were turned on demonstrators. German shepherds were used to scatter them.

Scenes like these dominated the news and the violence was horrifying. The reputations of numerous cities became such that tourism dried up, countrywide boycotts against national chains that discriminated in the South were carried out and tensions continued to mount.

As courts and the federal government imposed integration on state and local governments, the situation became untenable. Tokenism became a useful tool. Instead of forbidding integration, school districts would allow a few blacks into the school, allow a few blacks to register to vote, hire a few blacks to do menial jobs, ad nauseam. When the federal government threatened to withhold funds, such tactics served to qualify the local entities to receive federal support.

As mentioned in the previous chapter, when I was working in Tallahassee in 1965, Florida State University was seemingly totally white with no black students. However, one black undergraduate student attended classes with no fanfare. Even those of us in the heart of the civil rights movement had no notion of his presence in the student body. The existence of one black student there apparently defended FSU against being considered segregated but made little difference to the continuing segregation

Integration was impeded by violence against families that broke down barriers. Churches would be bombed, leaders like Medgar Evers were shot and killed in front of their homes in broad daylight and the perpetrators would not be prosecuted even though frequently everyone locally knew who they were.

Tokenism became a new wave for local officials and violence helped support the effort to keep the numbers low, thereby avoiding real integration. We will see numerous examples of this phenomenon throughout this book.

CHAPTER SIX

THE POLICE IN THE SOUTH

My father taught me to respect the police. Police were essential in keeping order in our communities. So long as I obeyed the law, they would not create any problems for me. I had very little personal contact with them. They knew me somewhat in Westbury, New York as an athlete on the school teams. I never got in trouble so there was no need for any interaction.

When out at night, there were times it was reassuring to see a police presence. I received a few speeding tickets and I was always polite. Sometimes they let me off with a promise to slow down. My experiences in college and in my first year in law school only served to reinforce my impression. My privileged lifestyle both kept me out of trouble and diminished any interaction with police personnel.

Going south, I did not expect any difference in attitude on either my part or theirs. I anticipated they would keep the peace as they did up north. When I learned that they did not take kindly to outside agitators telling them to make changes in their communities, it was confusing to me. Was that naïve? Unquestionably yes.

The odd thing here though was that my assignment was to try to have the law of our land enforced equally. I understood that was also what the police were charged to do. Hence, I imagined, there should be no conflict here.

What I failed to realize is that the police reflect the mores of the local community as well as the rule of law. They were there to preserve the society that they grew up in when they were asked to keep the peace. Typically, their educational level was similar to the majority of the people in their community. Often that meant no education beyond high school and limited experience outside of their community.

When the civil rights movement asked for changes in their southern cities and towns, practically without exception the police sided with keeping the status quo. City police chiefs and county sheriffs enforced the law in the manner with which they grew up. Segregation was part of that education.

Additionally, they were officials elected by the local population. If they were to demonstrate racial tolerance, even in the slightest, they would be thrown out of office in the next election. The deputies were chosen by the sheriffs and police chiefs. Typically, they came from the community where they worked and they were hired to maintain those communities as they found them: segregated and separate.

This dichotomy between enforcing the law and maintaining segregation, regardless of the law in many cases, was confusing to me. But it was simple for the local authorities. The status quo had to be maintained for local officials and their community, and their community included policemen.

By 1965, the law was clear: Segregation in public places was illegal. Access to institutions registered with local or federal governments had to serve all peaceful people seeking service, regardless of race. I was not in the South to make equal access happen. But I was charged with supporting those who did try to make that happen if they came to ask for legal aid.

In the following chapters there are numerous interactions with sheriffs, their deputies, and the local policemen. Most were very disturbing. When I was one-on-one with an officer of the law, I could have a civil conversation most of the time. But when there was a demonstration or police officers had taken a position not consistent with the law they were supposed to enforce, it was difficult to dialogue together. I was almost always polite and respectful, even if they did not act in a manner that deserved that respect.

I had some bad moments where their actions were truly egregious but in general, we were able to peacefully interact. But I was white and I was a lawyer in their minds. Black people doing similar jobs were treated differently and were barely tolerated.

Before I went to the South, I was only stopped by a police car for excessive velocity. In the South, I was only stopped because there was a black person in my car or because I was driving a car known to be owned by a black person in the community.

The contrast between the causes for my being pulled over was quite unsettling. You never knew what an officer, upset by racial issues, could be motivated to do. The fact that there were no recriminations for violating my rights made my position vulnerable. I was totally subject to the whims of a racist who did not take kindly to my presence in his community.

In today's world, unfortunately, similar attitudes are all too common. Most of our society is pretty much still segregated and often white police officers have had very little contact with black people, unless there is some suspicion of criminal activity. Many of them are fearful of violence when coming upon a black person, especially if he or she appears different from what the police person considers the norm.

Some cities have training for officers on how to deal with various situations and how to be racially sensitive. Police departments in smaller cities often do not have funds for such training.

Too many arrests for driving while black take place daily all over the country. Most end up with no issues and life goes on.

But many blacks are fed up with such treatment and may react emotionally. Such situations support the impression that racism is the norm, not the exception. Killings of innocent black people, arrests of innocent black people, will continue until there are more programs to train people about racial tolerance. The fact is that the major causes of death for black men is murder.

Blacks who live in desegregated communities tend to have fewer of these problems and police personnel who live in desegregated communities tend to have less encounters that result in racial problems. Cities and towns need to have interracial programs for kids, be it sports, be it arts and crafts or theatre, whatever. Integration breaks down barriers and helps reduce irrational fears of the other race.

CHAPTER SEVEN

SLAVERY, COTTON AND THE WORLD ECONOMY

In researching the impact of slavery on the economy of the United States, I discovered shocking facts about our country's history and the exploitation of blacks on the plantations of the southern states within the Union since the country's birth.

Cotton production and the subsequent textile production was the most important industry in the United States and Europe. King Cotton was the moniker used for the luxury product upon which the economy of the southern United States was based up to and even after the Civil War. The facts I will relate below makes one wonder how the North supported the Union's forces to eliminate slavery in our country as the textile industry was the most important sector of their economy.

Let us begin with some facts:

In the 1860s, cotton production was the most important part of the American economy. By most estimates it represented over 60% of the total economy. Furthermore, between 60% and 77% of American exports were cotton, mostly raw cotton for textile production in Great Britain. Economists compare the importance of cotton at this time to the position of oil in the 20th century! In fact, cotton was the leading export of the United States from 1803 to 1937! (Henry Louis Gates, Jr.)

Great Britain was the most important country in the world during the 19th century, both economically and militarily. Yet American cotton accounted for "over 80% of its essential industrial raw material. English textile mills accounted for 40% of Britain's exports. Twenty percent of Britain's population were directly or indirectly involved with cotton textiles." (Gene Dattel via Gates)

Additionally, the economy of the states of New England was dependent on the cotton production of the south. In the mid-1800s, 67% of the cotton used by mills in the U.S. was consumed in New England.

What was the basis of this most important world-wide industry? Black Slave Labor! The financial value of the slave labor was truly mind-boggling. It was as much a commodity as cotton itself with values that made it one of the most important economic assets in the country. For instance, according to the historian Steven Deyle, the total value of slaves in 1860 was equal to about seven times the value of all currency in circulation in the country and 48 times the total expenditure of the federal government! The richer the plantation owner, the more important was the value of the slaves in their possession. For instance, when Thomas Jefferson decided to build Monticello, his famous Virginia home, he mortgaged 150 slaves to guarantee the repayment of the loans he took from the banks.

That is absolutely astonishing. Hence the demand for more slaves was huge. It is no wonder that there was a move to create the Confederacy and for it to withdraw from the Union. Its entire economy depended upon slave labor and the existence of slave labor depended upon keeping blacks uneducated and without any civil rights to which the average citizen was entitled. That the north of the country wanted to change this system was an anathema to the south. Unquestionably, King Cotton was the fundamental cause of the Civil War, as slavery was fundamental to its continuing importance.

If we absorb the importance of cotton to the U.S. and world economy, we begin to comprehend the gravity and significance of abolitionist movement to free the slaves. Similarly, the Emancipation Proclamation and all of Abraham Lincoln's efforts to establish equality for these slaves takes on much greater meaning. At the end of the Civil War there were 500,000 slaves that were looking to start a new life and a broken confederacy of states looking for ways to make sure that this new freedom would not happen.

CHAPTER EIGHT

SLAVERY/SEGREGATION/DISCRIMINATION: REASONS WHY

The history about slavery, segregation and racial discrimination is riddled with puffery and false explanations of both their origin and justification. The fact is that the economy of colonial America and the country's first five decades were fueled by the exploitation of Native Americans initially, and by Negro submission secondly.

The economy of the southern states was fundamentally agricultural, with cotton being the major product as described in the previous chapter. Essential to making these investments profitable was the implementation of slave labor.

Religion and religious freedom were a fundamental part of life in the settlement and flourishing of the United States. Especially in the South, churches sprung up seemingly on every corner and much of the social life centered around them.

A basic tenet of Christian ethics as one of the Ten Commandments is "Do unto others as you would have them do unto you." Treat others as you would hope they would treat you. Exploitation of one's fellow man is a sin and violates the previously stated religious philosophy.

This created a fundamental cognitive dissonance for religious people who maintained slaves. A psychological resolution of this conflict was necessary for the country's survival. One could not be a good Christian and still exploit one's fellow man. Something had to give.

Make no mistake! The country's founders knew slavery was immoral and inhuman. Yet the farms of George Washington and Thomas Jefferson, inter alia, would not be economically viable if not for slave labor.

The psychological resolution of this conundrum was the invention that Negroes were sub-human, inferior to whites intellectually, and unable to survive on their own. Slavery would allow the poor Negro to survive as their white masters would give them a roof over their head and three meals a day, something they supposedly could not do on their own.

In order for this invention to take hold, Negroes could not be given opportunities in education or business where they could disprove this psychological construct. They had to work ungodly hours and then retire to their beds where they could rest and reproduce. They were treated much like horses and traded often as such. Prices were put on their proverbial heads and strong males were used as studs to increase the slave population and women were cultivated to work hard and reproduce often, not infrequently with the help of their owners.

Thus generations of whites and Negroes were born and raised with this thinking, even after slavery was outlawed after the Civil War. The culture of the South had this structure as fundamental teaching from birth to death. The dehumanization of the Negro, "... the underlying conception of man as a conveyable possession with no more autonomy of will and consciousness than a domestic animal" (David Brion Davis, *The Problem of Slavery in Western Culture*) was passed on from generation to generation resulting in a seemingly unchangeable conflict of values.

When a Negro was accused of theft, of sexual aggression, of being uppity, there was no pardon, no fair trial, no examination of the evidence.

A white woman's or white man's word against a Negro was sufficient in the South for the Negro to be hanged or jailed or beaten without a chance of defending himself. Their subjugation in this unfair world was justified because they were simply inferior. The all-white juries that heard these cases would believe the white accusers independent of common sense or other evidence. As previously discussed, the United States Supreme Court had handed down numerous decisions holding Negroes to be inferior and not equal citizens.

I had numerous conversations with racists throughout my young life and this perception of Negro inferiority was always in their thinking, sometimes subtly, most times overtly. Once I was discussing the football team of Florida State with the mayor of a small Florida town. He was a huge fan and went on about FSU's football history.

I wondered as to why they did not have an annual game against Florida A&M, the predominantly Negro university, also located in Tallahassee. It seemed so natural to me, as they would be crosstown rivals.

He assured me it would not be fair to the "nigras," as they could not stop the complicated plays FSU would put up. I mentioned that in the North, players like Jim Brown and Ernie Davis had become All-Americans and Heisman Trophy winners. I wondered if some day FSU might have Negro players. He acknowledged that Negroes were strong and ran well and could be linemen or receivers. But never a quarterback. They did not have the intellectual capacity to lead or follow complicated patterns.

Seventeen years passed and I revisited that same mayor on a trip with two of my kids around Florida. I reminded him of his thoughts on Negro quarterbacks, especially in light of Charlie Ward captaining FSU to a championship as a black quarterback and winning the Heisman Trophy.

He denied our entire conversation and said he never had any doubts about the Negroes' ability to play any position on the field. Cognitive dissonance did not allow him to keep this outmoded and clearly incorrect thinking, so his mind discarded what he had previously held to be fundamental to his thinking on race.

Hence, initially a racist created a psychological resolution of inferiority of the black race to justify slavery and their subjugation. Some racists cling to those opinions even today. Others, like the Floridian mayor cited above, discard their racism once they conclude that the facts totally reject their prior opinions on race relations.

Segregationists always had a choice as society changed. The most radical wanted things to remain the same, even in the face of new laws and Supreme Court decisions.

This attitude was symbolized by the government and powers that be in St. Augustine, Florida. In order for otherwise law-abiding citizens to cling to old-time segregation, which had come to be illegal under the civil rights laws of 1964, they would accuse those advocating change of being communists or anti-American.

They would avoid examining the issues raised by those seeking change; they would not opine on what is right or what is wrong. They would attempt to disqualify the demands of Dr. King and others striving for integration and equal rights by disqualifying them as individuals rather than dealing with the substance of what they were asking for.

We will examine the case of St. Augustine in great detail in the upcoming chapters but citing some facts here will be useful in understanding the issues under discussion in this chapter.

Sheriff Davis and Mayor Shelley from St. Augustine were examples of this type of attitude. They would never discuss whether the request for equal rights was reasonable or not. The sheriff would not address with me whether the impossible suicide in his jail was possible. It was a fait accompli, no longer up for discussion.

Mayor Shelley would never meet with Dr. Martin Luthur King or discuss his demands. He would never opine as to whether more jobs for Negroes was a reasonable request or whether Negro students should or should not be allowed to attend formerly white schools. He would attack those making those requests as outside agitators trying to undo the history of the oldest city in the country, change what all its citizens preferred over the years. Communists! Anti-American! But never discussing whether the civil rights leaders' demands were right or wrong.

The use of the words nigger or nigra were/are part and parcel of the classification of blacks as subhuman, inferior. Poor whites in the South had the consolation that they were not inferior, that they were not niggers.

The repetition of the word enabled them to have a self-image of being at least better than blacks. It was little consolation for their sad fate but it was something that they did not want to relinquish.

Ku Klux Klan meetings reinforced this mindset. Keeping blacks out of their schools, keeping facilities separate or "colored," as the public signs used to demand — all of this fed the need for poor whites to be on a social level better than blacks. None of this was easy to give up. Segregationist leaders knew this and appealed to it.

Unfortunately, poor whites never focused on the problems they shared with poor blacks. The tribal identification of being white erased the economic ties poor people should identify with and try to change together.

It was no accident that St Augustine's Sheriff Davis was reelected with over 70% of the vote in the 1960s. Sheriff Davis referred to blacks as "nigras". He went into Lincolnville, an important predominantly black neighborhood, and spoke directly to the "nigras" before his reelection. "Don't vote for me, you nigras!" he would shout on his loudspeaker while driving through the streets.

The use of the word "nigra" both showed his opinion that blacks were inferior as well separating himself from the poorer racists who used "nigger" to refer to blacks. In his mind, he was a kinder, gentler racist leader who could be somewhat considerate to blacks who were respectful of the norms of St. Augustine and were not "uppity."

We look back on his reign from 1949 to 1970 with regret as he stood strong to maintain the racism and segregation that dominated the town of St. Augustine against the new laws that had been passed that legalized integration and outlawed segregation.

Although he was quoted as saying he would uphold these new laws in practice, nothing changed during his years in office and eventually the then-governor, Claude Kirk, removed him and replaced him with a new sheriff. We look back on those years and his overwhelming reelection with shock that the overall population supported his racist actions.

In November 2018, the election for Florida's governor had a black

Democratic Party candidate lose to a conservative Republican who made unfortunate comments that were seemingly racially motivated. This Republican garnered 72% of the votes in the rural Northern Florida counties, including, but not limited to, that of St. John's County where St. Augustine is the county seat.

The total statewide difference between the candidates was less than 1% but the northern counties that did not have medium or large cities still have the same overwhelming rejection of a black candidate that 1965 had.

Old habits are hard to break. Generations that have been brought up being taught that blacks are sub-human, rapists, animals, lazy, smelly, etc. do not change easily. When politicians use certain racist keywords, they trigger certain reactions for people who still oppose racial equality. In my mind, one thing is for sure: This type of communication works. A proverbial "slip of the tongue" is enough for rural whites to know that the candidate is "one of us" and their vote is secure.

Donald Trump did that successfully as did the Republican governor of Florida when he said the state does not want the "same old monkey business." The more he repeated that this was not meant to be racist, the more the message got out to his public that he was on their racist side.

As his black Democratic opponent said, "I am not saying he is racist, I am saying, though, that all the racists are supporting him."

CHAPTER NINE

NIGGER, NIGRA, NEGRO

The above words appear throughout this book as they were all commonly used in the South in the 1960s.

"Nigger" is a horrible word on numerous levels. Historically, its most powerful usage has been by white racists in reference to black people. It is a put-down of the lowest level. No matter how poor or unfortunate a white person was, he could console himself by considering himself superior to a nigger. A racist wanted the black people to be considered lower-level humans and the word nigger was a forceful reminder, in their minds, that blacks were sub-human.

The usage of this word was shockingly common, especially in the Southern United States up to and throughout the 1960s. The word nigger incorporates hatred and a desire on the part of non-blacks to forbid any decent treatment of black people on any level, the campaign to keep them under the heel of their "superiors." I have seen this word spit out by racists in the meanest, most disparaging manner and it is scarred in my memory as to how horrific its usage is.

That said, I object to the people, especially reporters, referring to the word "nigger" as the "N word" when addressing its usage. Saying the "N word" in lieu of saying "nigger" softens the impact of the horror of the word.

If someone uses this word, it should be quoted as in "So and So called him a nigger" not "So and So called him the "N word." Hearing the word nigger in a report shocks the senses and it should. Hearing "the N word" is troublesome, but is much less bothersome than the word itself and should be quoted directly in order for the usage to have its full, revolting impact on the listener.

In my conversations with sheriffs and other people of authority while in the South, I noticed they often used the word nigra, which clearly is a variation on the word nigger. While its usage is somewhat softer than nigger, nigra does incorporate the sense that blacks are inferior to the rest of them. It is just a gentler form, perhaps, of the same meaning. Nigger has a sense of enemy to it. If one might say "He is a good nigger," he probably means he does not make waves, does what he is told.

Nigra is used to refer to blacks as inferior but the speaker wants to show he tolerates them. Nigger implicitly states that the speaker believes that the black man is subhuman and intolerable. We should call it like it is and get angry that someone used it in normal speech. Fundamental to repeated usage is the desire of the speakers to remind one and all of who is in charge. The put-down incorporated in the usage of this language reinforces the thinking that the white man runs the show and the black man is subordinate to white superiority.

Until 1968, blacks were referred to as Negroes. Dr. King never accepted the term "black"as a substitution. The race was Negro, which had no pejorative sense to it. Even Afro-American was not used.

In 1968, Stokely Carmichael made an epic speech after James Meredith, the first black to attend the University of Mississippi, was shot. He excoriated the racism throughout the country and denounced non-violence and the term Negro as being part of the white culture. He praised the Black Panthers for physically protecting other blacks and declared that his race was the black race and raised a fist to symbolize his new mantra of "Black Power."

This thinking and these terms struck a chord with young black people and many others, both black and white. His words were soon generally adopted and the use of the term Negro gradually diminished until recent years when it fell into virtual total disuse.

That said, I use the term Negro often in this book which I feel reflects the time I am talking about, the mid-1960s. It is to give a feeling of the time that the civil rights movement was at its peak. It is not meant to be, nor do I believe it is in any way, disrespectful to black people. Sometimes it is used herein interchangeably with "black" folks.

One of the saddest aspects of the word nigger is how its usage separates the poor white person from the poor black person. Economically, poor whites and poor blacks have the same interests and should have the same goals. They should, it would seem, want to better their financial and educational situations. They should, it would seem, want to have the government help give them a chance to use their abilities to better themselves through work and through school.

Yet, when whites take solace in putting down their fellow blacks, just because of the color of the latter's skin, and despite their similar problems and needs, they only serve to reduce their own potential, as an economic class, for change.

Hence, the feeling of an almost tribal fixation of the poor white being part of a superior class, despite having so little of his or her own, has been stronger than economic realities. This has a reflection so visible in our country even today when we examine the issue of health care. Poor whites tend to be against Obamacare, which they desperately need, in part because they view it as a handout to poor blacks. As politicians have realized much earlier than their followers, the poor will follow their perceived values, however self-defeating, rather than their obvious economic interests.

In part, sadly, in my opinion, this self defeating thinking by under privileged southern whites is a major reason why many of the poorest states in the country are in the Deep South.

CHAPTER TEN

VIOLENCE AND THE THREAT OF VIOLENCE IN THE 1960s

In the 1960s, when new legislation was passed and when judges began to lay down rulings forcing integration, the frustration that segregationists felt often resulted in illegal violent acts against people trying to enter previously segregated schools, hotels, restaurants, as well as those blacks leading voter registration drives. Historically, such violent acts went unpunished in the southern states. Before the Civil War, there was no protection for blacks in the south. All land/slave owners ruled over their own blacks as they saw fit. Physical abuse and brutality kept the slaves under their control.

After the Civil War, emancipated slaves began to have freedom and individual achievements on many levels. When President Andrew Johnson allowed the white landowners to regain control and the southern states were allowed to rejoin the Union, outrageous savagery against blacks ended all progress and the power structure once again became all white. These vicious onslaughts prevailed through the end of the 19th century and into the 20th century.

In the 1950s, and especially in the 1960s, these physical attacks became well known as television and written journalism made everyone a witness. It is difficult to describe the fear that such violence or threats of violence created in the minds of those striving to desegregate. Among many others, the killings such as that of Medgar Evers in Mississippi in the driveway of his home or that of the three civil rights workers in Philadelphia, Mississippi in 1964 had a seriously terrifying effect on people in the movement.

The fact is that rampages against blacks were commonplace after the post-Civil War period in the effort to combat the attempts of the black population to exercise the rights acquired through legislation and the passage of important amendments to the constitution. Hangings and mass shootings were the most notorious and therefore the most chilling acts of inhumanity brought upon the black population.

The threat of unprovoked attacks were constant and were made even worse by the fact that most of the civil rights movements used non-violence to accentuate the horrors of segregation. Ku Klux Klan rallies brought in speakers, both local and national, who exhorted their followers to commit atrocities and to praise previous ones. Typically, although not always, the people who were the most easily influenced to carry out vicious attacks were poorly educated and of low economic means. Keeping black citizens down was essential for their psychological well-being, as they had little else to celebrate.

Key to the unrestrained atrocities committed against blacks was the total lack of potential criminal justice against the perpetrators of this brutality. The local police were sympathetic, if not totally approving, of the aggressive acts against blacks. Rarely were racists prosecuted for what they did to blacks and if, by some odd coincidence, a white was charged with a crime for attacking a black person, the judge and jury were typically as racist as the accused criminal and nothing happened under the law.

Crowds that gathered to protest the integration of beaches or schools got riled up by the threat that such locations would be integrated and these crowds were easily manipulated to take the law into their own hands. As Jimmy Jackson, a civil rights activist, told me in St. Augustine, "When we were in our early twenties we thought we were invincible."

We took monumental risks in confronting segregationists in the effort to achieve integration. In reliving some of my experiences in Florida in 1965, I would get chills while thinking of what could have happened but fortunately did not.

When Judge Bryan Simpson ordered the motel owners and restaurant owners of St. Augustine to integrate or get fined, these managers were in a very difficult position. If they refused, they would be fined and would lose money. If they integrated, they would be exposed to attacks on their properties, the damage of which could be even greater than their potential fines.

The manager of the Monson Motor Lodge in St. Augustine had damage of some $3,000 in 1964 when he followed Judge Simpson's order to allow blacks in his restaurant. No one was punished for causing the damage, as the authorities were against said integration.

When a church was bombed or a grenade was thrown into a private house of a civil rights leader, the crimes were not even investigated, much less punished. Dr. King's rented home in St. Augustine was firebombed and destroyed in the summer of 1964. No investigation into who was responsible for these acts was ever even initiated. The lack of police interest in preventing such violence only incentivated the perpetrators to continue to use violence as a way of preventing integration.

Another important factor was that most of the demonstrations happened in the summer when northern students came south on their school summer breaks. The local people knew that they would return to the North at the end of August and the local blacks would be left alone to fend for themselves. The threat of violence was more extreme then, as the newspaper reporters frequently would leave as well, since they expected little to happen starting in September. So the glare of national attention to acts of brutality would be minimum without reporters present.

When SCLC removed their people from St. Augustine in August of 1964, all of the press went with them and the continuing efforts of local blacks in the integration effort was met with more repression that went totally unnoticed nationally. Hoss Manucy, the local Klan leader in St. Augustine, and his cohorts had free rein and the segregation of the restaurants and hotels returned in full force.

In January 1965, Harper's Magazine described St. Augustine's situation as anarchy. "The city's institutions of law and order have cracked under the strain .... its terrorists have adopted new tactics .... after an orgy of ... summer violence ....The worst is the silent fear of ordinary men who know their lives depend on avoiding the threatened night ambushes, the Molotov cocktails, and the sniper attacks."

They went on to quote a local white resident, "We have taken a $7 million loss in the tourist trade ....There is this uneasiness you feel every time some nigger gets beaten up .... You can't help thinking you might be next."

This article, which carefully described the happenings in St. Augustine up to January 1965, when it was published, went on to say, "One is finally driven to conclude that much of what happened in St. Augustine flowed from a simple belief held by a large number of influential people: They could 'beat the niggers' if they kept the heat on long enough. In a sense the 'heat' is still on, but now there are new considerations; the dead, the scarred, and the scared---and an awful legacy of bitterness."

Essential to the efforts of segregationists to maintain "their way of life" was the overhanging threat of violence which was made more real by occasional actual acts of serious attacks in the community. But St. Augustine teaches us that such atrocities can serve to delay justice but will not stop justice.

CHAPTER ELEVEN

COURAGE

As we reflect on the various chapters in the civil rights movement that is now a part of the history of the United States, especially for people too young to have lived through those complicated times, it is never redundant to remind ourselves of how much courage was necessary to achieve the victories, step by step, inch by inch, day by day, of the process to attain equal rights for the people of color.

Just imagine being dedicated to the use of non-violence to emphasize the dehumanizing, systematic discrimination faced by blacks throughout the South when there are scores of seething, white segregationists carrying baseball bats and worse, supported by police with water hoses, angry German shepherds and billy sticks waiting to confront you.

It is one thing to face an enemy with equal arms in a battle. That requires courage. However, to go into a battle ready to be beaten in order to show the nation the horrors of segregation under the circumstances outlined above requires courage of a much greater level, with a dedication to the cause that is difficult to fully appreciate.

In my time in the South, I needed to be brave for certain moments of conflict with the powers that were willing to take severe action in order to preserve the segregation that they had grown up with and wished to maintain. But what I did was a small fraction of what so many others did for decades.

For instance, let us examine the path taken by John Lewis, then of Alabama and now a Georgia congressman. John Lewis in 1960, at the age of 21, led non-violent sit-ins in Nashville, Tennessee, where he was met with beatings by the local police. The local restaurants were segregated and did not want to change this 'tradition.'

He organized and led the original Freedom Rides. As one of the original 13 Riders, seven whites and six blacks, Lewis traveled by bus from Washington, D.C. to New Orleans, meeting major violence and bus burning along the way. This led to the Boynton ruling that outlawed segregated buses for interstate travel.

Lewis was arrested multiple times and beaten frequently, yet he kept coming back in order to change the systematic segregation that was then prevalent there.

He organized "Freedom Summer" in Mississippi to register black people to vote, where he was repeatedly beaten and his life was threatened. He organized bus boycotts in various cities across the South. He was hated by Southern sheriffs and mayors and other civil rights leaders feared for his life. Nothing slowed him down.

In 1963 he was chosen to head SNCC, the most radical of the important civil rights organizations. By that point, his courage was greatly respected by everyone in the civil rights movement. He had been beaten numerous times and arrested 24 times. He was the youngest, at 23, of "the big six leaders" who organized the March on Washington, where Dr. King gave his monumental "I Have a Dream" speech. He is the only survivor at this time of those leaders and those speakers of that historic march.

Perhaps he is most remembered as one of the leaders of the march to cross the Edmund Pettus Bridge in Selma, Alabama where he was savagely beaten and almost killed by the mounted police as national TV carried the horrific carnage of the infamous "Bloody Sunday" of March 7, 1965.

The bravery exhibited throughout his life by John Lewis exceeds any words I could use here to extol what he has achieved. As an active, yet older man today, he bears multiple scars from those efforts. As a person who confronted comparatively minor incidents with police and racist counter-demonstrators, I have unbridled admiration and respect for the courage that has highlighted his life and his accomplishments.

Similarly, other leaders and thousands of brave followers confronted violence and threats and beatings, yet came back over and over to achieve integration of the schools and voter rolls, as well as job opportunities for all races.

This movement required the relentless efforts of thousands of dedicated volunteers who believed in a goal to change their country, to right the wrongs of numerous generations. It was very difficult, is very difficult, and required(s) courage and dedication to a cause that was so meaningful to all of those involved. I am humbled to have played a minor role during the summer of 1965.

CHAPTER 12

MARIANNA, FLORIDA

After some three weeks living and working in Tallahassee with John Due, Esq., he deemed me ready for my first case. About 10 a.m. one morning, Mr. Due called me into his office.

"You ready to go out and investigate a case for me, son?"

"I sure am," I replied, displaying more anxiety than I normally did.

"I was just called to defend a Negro man who has been charged with attempted rape of a white girl in Marianna. I need you to go out and speak to him and find out what happened."

"OK. When do I go?"

"Now. He will pick you up at the bus station in Marianna. Ira will drop you off at the station. The bus leaves in 45 minutes. Here is some money to get you there and back. Have some lunch too. Bring receipts. Good luck. Don't get in trouble."

I got into the car with Ira Simmons, who was, like me, going into his second year in law school. He had graduated from Florida A&M and was now going to law school at Howard University in Washington, D.C.

In 1965, Florida colleges were completely segregated. Florida State University (FSU), located in Tallahassee, was the largest state university in Florida. With the exception of one token Afro-American undergraduate student and two token graduate students, the student body had no members of color. In an earlier chapter, I discussed in detail the use of tokenism by segregationist governments and this trickery, unknown to the general public, allowed the segregated colleges to pass as integrated. Florida A&M was the "separate but equal" black university, also located in Tallahassee.

Ira warned me to be careful. "Marianna is a cracker town. Don't be a hero there. Stay low. Rape cases are the worst. Don't go to the police station or the courthouse. There will be no cooperation and you could run into some non-welcoming folks."

With that orientation, he dropped me off at the bus station, where I bought a one-way Greyhound ticket to Marianna.

When I got on the bus, I sat in the front row so I could have an unobstructed view of the road ahead and maybe get a little bit of a feel for the region. Naively, I forgot that the buses were de facto segregated and blacks mostly sat in the back.

Later, as a matter of principle I would sit in the back. In fact, interstate bus lines had been desegregated by a Supreme Court decision as early as 1946. But the ruling did not address intrastate travel at the time and total resolution of the issue was not given any real force until many years later.

On the multiple bus trips I took in Florida, I did not see any problem if a white sat in the back or a black sat in the front.

At the time, I did not know that Florida is the flattest state in the country. The I-10 road going west from Tallahassee is as flat and straight as it could be. Marianna is 65 miles directly west of Tallahassee and seemingly without even a minor hill. Marianna is 167 feet above sea level.

In 1965, its population was slightly more than 7,000 people. In 2010, it was slightly more than 6,000. In 2017, the population was estimated to be a little over 7,000. Draw your own conclusions about the town's attractions.

Marianna is a town whose sole purpose seemingly is to allow the crossing of two highways, U.S. Route 90 and Interstate 10. My bus was taking Interstate 10, which travels to Pensacola, Florida, and on to Louisiana and Mississippi.

Let me assure you that the culture of all these locations was similar. Florida was as racist and dangerous to African Americans as the other places along I-10. In 1965, these states were part of what were called the "Black Belt" states.

Beginning in Mississippi, they stretched across to Florida and up through Virginia. The initial reason for this name was the fertile black soil that made the above-mentioned stretch. However, with the prevalence of slave labor that enabled the farms along this stretch to be profitable, principally the cotton farms, the Black Belt came to refer to farming areas using slave labor.

Marianna was founded in 1828 by a Scottish entrepreneur, Scott Beverege, who named the town after his daughters, Mary and Anna. The area was home to many farms, most of which existed as a result of cheap labor offered by slavery.

U.S. Route 90 comes from the Southwest and becomes the main street of Marianna before continuing in a northerly direction. Lafayette Street, as it is called in town, houses most of Marianna's important buildings.

Its official nickname is "The City of Southern Charm." Someone had a sarcastic sense of humor in so naming it. Its history is typical of small, Black Belt towns with little discernible charm. Its main economy was centered around agriculture.

John Milton was an owner of a large plantation in Marianna and hundreds of slaves. During the Civil War, he was elected governor of Florida. As a firm believer that the Confederacy should not rejoin the Union, he vowed that he would die before he would agree to said unification. He was outspoken in his defense of slavery and the southern "way of life." When Union troops approached Tallahassee on April 1, 1865 to effect unification, the governor kept his promise and shot himself while on his plantation. He is buried in Marianna.

Marianna was the site of a massacre during the beginning of the Civil War where some 150-200 Republicans, many black men, were murdered by members of the KKK. The massacre was spurred by land disputes, most of which involved land owned by blacks.

Violence marked Marianna's existence, principally over preventing blacks from any meaningful presence in the local economy. Lynchings in northern Florida were the highest in the country on a per capita basis.

In 1934, the brutal lynching of Claude Neal, a black man accused of rape and murder, attracted countrywide attention to Marianna. The KKK attempted to forcefully expel all black residents of Marianna, forcing the governor to call in the National Guard to restore peace. Over 200 blacks and some police were injured. The white vigilantes leading the uprising were never named nor indicted.

Marianna housed the Florida School for Boys—originally called the Florida State Reform School, at one point The Industrial School for Boys and in its latter years the Dozier School for Boys—from 1900 to 2011. It was segregated until 1967 and for many years it was the largest juvenile reform institution in the country.

Reports from black youths held there tell stories of being treated like slaves under even worse abuse than their white compatriots, including after the school was desegregated. They were forced to work in the fields planting, with proceeds going to the state, rather than being taught a trade and lived in more squalid conditions.

During this time, it gained the reputation as one of the worst locations for abuse, beatings, rape, torture and even murder by its staff. Numerous investigations were conducted and changes in administration occurred but the abuse continued. Finally, mercifully, the institution was closed after 111 sorrowful years.

An investigation by the University of South Florida in 2012 cited secret details of a dungeon where boys under 12 were repeatedly raped and otherwise sexually abused. Fifty-five bodies were discovered there, most of which were outside the cemetery grounds. The multiple charges of abuse were confirmed by investigations conducted by The Florida Department of Law Enforcement in 2010 and by the Civil Rights Division of the U.S. Justice Department in 2011.

In 1964, two Negro boys were sent to the "school" by a local judge in St. Augustine for demonstrating against segregation. It was a horrendous display of racism and it is fully discussed in the chapter about St. Augustine.

Today, Marianna hosts the Federal Correctional Institution, a medium-security United States federal prison for male inmates, with a population of 1,300. A minimum-security female prison is adjacent. The government and the private administrator of the men's prison have been defendants in various lawsuits by inmates and guards for unsafe and health-damaging policies.

The drive was uneventful, with little natural beauty. When we stopped in Marianna, there was a rather tall, maybe 6'4," very muscular gentleman waiting for me. For different reasons, we both stood out from the rest of the people, less than a dozen, at the stop. He stood out because he was a strapping, physically impressive black man. I stood out because I was clearly socializing with him. Doing so in public was not looked upon kindly by the white population there.

We got into a red and white Chevrolet, with huge fins from the late 1950s. John spoke in a surprisingly quiet voice for such a big guy and seemed naturally shy.

"Let's go to my house so we can talk about the case."

"Sounds good to me. Is there a date for the trial?"

"Yessir. Next Tuesday."

"Hmm", I mumbled. "I guess there is not a heavy caseload here."

"That's right. This is a serious problem for me though. 'Cause if I am convicted, I lose my job. I'm a cook for the city. It is a good job for me. I have a wife and kids. I don't know what I can do if I lost it."

That did not make me feel good. I didn't want to be responsible for John losing his job.

John lived in a nice house in a Negro neighborhood. He had a small lawn and the house was nondescript. But it was clean outside and very neat inside. He introduced his wife, who was quite young, probably younger than me, and she carried two kids; a baby and what seemed to me to be a two-year old. After she gave me a glass of water, they went to another room.

I looked at John as if to say, tell me what happened.

After what seemed like a pause that lasted forever, he spoke. "It is not a very interesting story. I was driving east on I -10. On the edge of town, a car stopped in front of me to make a left into a drive-in hamburger place. Most of the white teenagers hung out there at night. Even after the oncoming cars passed, she didn't make the turn. There was no way for me to go around her.

"She later said I blinked my lights at her. The two girls in the car looked back at me and then turned into the hamburger place and I went on down the road. About five minutes later, a cop car was flashing his lights and motioning me to pull over."

John rubbed his large hands together nervously. Sweat broke out above his top lip. There was an awkward pause.

"The cop opened my door and yelled at me to get out of the car. 'Don't give me any guff, nigger,' he yelled. He told me to turn around and put my hands behind my back. When I did, he handcuffed me. Then he swung me around and punched me in my face. I could feel blood dripping out of my nose. He put me in the back of his police car and drove me to the drive-in.

"By now, there was a lot of blood coming out of my nose and it covered my mouth and chin. I couldn't wipe it 'cause my hands were cuffed behind my back. He called two girls over and asked them if this was the nigger that tried to rape them. They nodded in agreement.

"Then he put his face in front of mine. 'You won't get away with this, nigger. There is justice in Marianna. Let's go.'

"Then he pushed me towards his car and took me down to get indicted.

Since I worked for the city, they let me go and gave me this paper."

He handed me a legal paper from the Marianna Courthouse that said he was caught trying to rape two girls and that his trial would be at 11 a.m. the next Tuesday.

Then it hit me. I was 22, privileged and naive as hell. What was I going to do to help this guy?

As if on cue, John asked, "What are you going to do?"

I hoped I didn't look puzzled or scared. "I need to get some facts, John. We need to find some people to corroborate your story."

"OK, man. Take my car. I can't work today so I will stay here."

He gave me his keys and told me how to get to the drive-in. It was well after 11 a.m. and it should be open. Within a few minutes, I made the same left the girls had made into the drive-in.

The gravel seemed to crunch under the car's tires. The parking was spacious in front of a red wooden building. A string of multi-colored lights hung off the eaves of the roof. They seemed like leftover Christmas lights and did not add nor subtract from the drab look of the hamburger place.

I was the only car there. Yet no one came out to take my order. I rolled down the window. In a few minutes a lady in an ecru uniform came out and said hi. She wore white, low-cut sneakers and her skirt ended below her knees. I said hi back.

She said, "Nice car. Is it yours?"

"Why do you ask that?"

She hesitated. She looked at me for a while, silently. I looked back. Hopefully there was going to be some good conversation eventually.

Finally she spoke. "You look like a good guy, someone I can talk to. Not a lot of people like that around here. You are not from around here, I am quite sure of that."

Among things that were different between us was her heavy drawl. After four years of college in the Midwest, my New York accent was very moderated but clearly not southern.

I nodded as if to say she was correct and I was not from around here. It did not come as a shock to her.

"This car. Whose is it?"

"Why is that important?"

"Well, there was a colored with a car that looked like that. Coloreds don't come in here, ya see. When you pulled up I thought it might be him."

"Can I order something to eat?

She smiled. "I'm so sorry!" she said. "How stupid of me. What would you like?"

"How about your best burger, some fries and a Ginger Ale?"

"I'll get it right away."

"Listen, I like talking to you. After you put in the order, come back and we can continue."

She smiled and nodded and ran into the shop to make the order.

Shortly she was back. She seemed relieved of a burden and came up to my car. John's car, that is.

"So if Negroes don't come in here, why was his car here?"

"Well, Buster, one of the local cops, brought his car here and then brought a big colored here from the station so he could go home. He was really bloody and ... well, it caused a big commotion. Everyone was looking at the big guy with blood pouring down his face. They didn't even give him a towel or paper to clean himself. Buster took off his cuffs. The colored just got in the car and drove away."

"Did Buster say what happened?"

"Yeah. See there are two sisters who are always here, if you know what I mean. They had said the colored had tried to rape them and Buster ... well, Buster is not much of a ladies man, ya see. He went after the colored. He wanted to show he was tough, ya know ....

"Look---he wanted to show off to these girls. So he brought the big colored guy back here all bloody and made them say whether this guy was the guy who bothered them. They said yes and Buster took him down to the station, I guess. When he came back Chipper and the colored were with him. They went to get this car, I'm guessing it was this car, and the colored got in it and drove away.

"What exactly did the Negro man do to the girls?"

The woman looked at me, as if to say, 'seriously?' "Well, he must have done something to deserve to get punched out by Buster!"

She let out a deep breath. "Let me get your food."

She came back with a big roll with a small, overcooked hamburger patty and some undercooked fries.

"Sweetie. Are you going to tell me what the Negro man did to deserve getting punched?"

My voice indicated this was a serious discussion.

"He didn't do anything. These girls, let's say, hang out here every night."

"And so what?"

"I mean they are always here,"

"I get that. This is their hangout. What is wrong with that?' I asked.

"OK. You are not getting my drift. They make money here. They do stuff with guys and get paid. Look over there."

She pointed further down the parking lot which extended some 30 yards away. I looked. Then I looked back at her. I shrugged my shoulders and lifted the palms of my hands up, as if to say 'so'?

"That part of the parking does not have lights. They get into a guy's car and he drives down there. Got it?"

I nodded. "And Buster wanted some of that?"

She nodded.

I asked her name and she gave it to me. I asked her for her telephone number but she shook her head negatively.

"Do the girls live nearby?"

"Up in the Caverns. They rent there."

"Caverns? Seriously?"

She laughed. "That's the name of the state park, Florida Caverns. It is right up that road. A few miles north. After you enter the park, make your first left. You will see a small cabin a little ways up. It is in a wooded area. You won't miss it. Nothing else around there."

Florida Caverns State Park is part of the Florida State Parks system. Today it is a standout of "Florida's Natural Wonders." It is the only cavern system open to the public in the state.

Being that Florida is the flattest state in the country, it is hard to imagine that there would be a series of connected caverns to visit. This is especially true as Florida also has the highest percentage of wetlands of any state in the continental United States. This would make flooding a natural happening.

Nevertheless, these caves are a fascinating natural attraction. There are many details about this park that make it unique that I subsequently discovered but are not relevant for this story.

Not only was having a state park of caverns odd and surprising, it seemed even odder that people who had nothing to do with the park were living there in a house. Marianna was a seemingly sleepy town full of surprises for me.

"Thanks. I am going to try and see them. How long will you be here?"

"I get off at 3. Got to get home to my kids."

"I really want to talk more to you. I need you to testify. You are too nice a person. You won't let an innocent man get convicted and lose his job. He has a wife and kids."

"Not a chance of that. I would lose my job. My husband would beat me up. My friends won't see me. I can't have any of that. I will help you but I won't talk in front of a judge. No way."

I was ringing wet. John was totally screwed; if she wouldn't testify, those girls wouldn't either. Not sure what options I had.

I gave her the dirty plates and paid the bill with a big tip. She smiled a smile of gratitude.

"I'm really sorry. Even a colored does not deserve to go to jail for something he didn't do."

"Well, I won't be here tomorrow but I need to talk to you. I'll come back another day. The trial is Tuesday. Please think about helping out."

"What's your name?"

"Frank"

"'Bye, Frank. Good luck."

She turned with the dirty plates and walked away. I started the car engine and went north up the small dirt road off I-10.

The waitress was correct. I couldn't miss the small cabin as there was nothing but trees and gravel around the area. I pulled into an area about 10 feet from the cabin. A curtain in a window moved as if to allow a person to look out.

I walked up to the front door. I knocked but there was no response. I waited. It was very hot. The end of June in northern Florida. Must have been in the 90s. I wiped my face on my sleeve and knocked again. Someone looked out the window. Still nothing.

"Come on," I called out. "I just want to talk. No one wants trouble."

The door opened. Two girls looked out at me. They seemed to relax a bit when they saw I was alone and white. At least, that is what I presumed after my last experience. This car was like a spotlight flashing trouble.

"Hi," I said brightly.

They smiled and told me to come in. They had a small table and some chairs and offered for me to sit down.

The girls were older than me, maybe late twenties. One was heavyset with messy hair. She was more reserved. The other was very attractive with a curvaceous figure and a beautiful face with bright, clean skin. I would have never guessed she was doing tricks in a drive-in burger joint. She looked me up and down and smiled broadly.

"What do you want from us?" she asked, perhaps a little too coyly.

"Right now I just want to talk. I guess you recognized the car I am driving."

They nodded. They were apprehensive. I was choosing my words carefully so as not to make the situation more tense than it already was.

"Look. The car's owner is going to trial next week for attempted rape. He has a wife and two kids. If he gets convicted, he is out in the street with no job. He has no money saved up. His kids will have no food. Is this what you want to happen?'

They both gulped. "Jeez," said the good-looking one. "No! That wouldn't be fair."

I looked very seriously at her. We all had our private thoughts.

I spoke next. "What exactly happened that night that led to his being arrested?"

"Well, ya know, the burger place is our hangout. We are there almost every night. We were on 10 going to drive into the parking lot but there was a lot of traffic. We waited for the oncoming cars to pass. All of a sudden the car behind us starts flashing his lights.

"We looked back and saw this big colored guy. I got really scared and drove into the parking lot. One of the cops, Buster, was there. He is always after me and I was crying. He asked me what happened and I told him. So Buster goes after the colored.

"After a while, he is back with the colored in his car and the lights are flashing and the siren is ringing. He calls me over and asks me if this is the nigger that tried to rape me. I never said he tried to rape me. But it was scary and I nodded my head that it was him. The colored was bleeding from his nose. Then Buster takes off with the colored."

She paused for a deep breath. I looked at her expectantly. The temporary silence seemed deafening. Her sister shifted uncomfortably in her chair.

"We all drank some soda and waited, wondering when Buster would get back and what he would tell us. Most of the guys wanted blood. They wanted Buster to bring the colored back and let them deal with him. I did not know what to think. I just wanted to have some fun and forget what happened.

"In a while, Buster came back with another cop and the colored and the colored's car. The colored was still bleeding from the nose. His shirt was covered in blood. Buster pulled him out of the car. He was a big colored and he stared at me. His hands were behind his back. The guys were yelling at him, telling Buster to let them have him.

"Buster told them to calm down. 'We will let justice take care of this nigger. His trial is Tuesday. Just let it go for now.' Then he took off the colored's cuffs and told him to go home. So the colored got in his car and drove off."

The other sister joined in. "Why are you driving the nigger's car?"

This sister was a little cruder than her sister, I concluded. The first sister used a "polite" pejorative for Negro. Her sister had no such reservations. She questioned me. "Why are you here? Why do you care?"

"He is in big trouble. His trial is coming up and if he is convicted he will lose his job and his wife and kids---well, they will have no food, no shelter. Nothing. All that for flicking his lights. Do you think that is fair? I work for a lawyer in Tallahassee that he called for help. I am here to try and straighten this out. To do that I need your help."

The good-looking sister started to cry. At first, tears started flowing. Soon she seemed to lose her breath. She was shaking her head, trying to talk but was losing it. I got up and patted her on her back, urging her to relax.

"We will figure this out. Just try to get a grip."

She started to breathe somewhat normally. "I am scared."

There was silence. I looked at the other sister. She looked away. I tried to size up how to proceed. I waited.

"This is all Buster's fault," the other sister blurted. "He wants some action from her, goddamn it. He is such a sleaze. He doesn't want to pay … thinks a cop is better than the others.

"Now he gets us in this shit with a nigger. We never said he did anything. We just got scared. We just thought the nigger wanted something from us, ya know. Got us scared. When we looked back we thought it would be a friend flashing at us. When we saw the nigger, we freaked. Then Buster created this goddamn mess. What are we gonna do now?"

It was hotter than hell in that cabin. No breeze, no A/C. Our situation didn't help. I was soaked in sweat. I tried to keep a poker face, but my mind was racing. I knew I had to leave there with a solution.

"OK, OK. I think from what you both are saying that my client, John, in fact did not try to rape you. In fact, he never even touched you nor did he try to. It was all just a misunderstanding. Is that correct?"

"Yes, yes. That's it. Just a misunderstanding!" They were nodding and repeating, "Just a misunderstanding."

"OK," I said. "OK."

Pausing, I took a deep breath and let it out slowly. "But I think you do not want this, um, misunderstanding to make John lose his job and not be able to feed his family. Right?"

They nodded vigorously. "Yeah, wouldn't be fair to the nigger," the other sister proffered. "He didn't do anything really."

I suggested we write down a statement for each of them and they could sign it. The statements would basically reflect what they had just said and that everything was just a misunderstanding in the heat of the moment. They found some paper and motioned to me to start writing.

Each declaration was dated that day and described the incident blandly. They admitted they were scared when they saw it was a Negro in the car behind them, but in fact, he never left his car and never even said anything to them. In sum, there was no attempted rape.

Each printed their names on their respective statements and then signed it. They then suggested we all get a beer. I begged off. I told them I didn't drink and, anyway I had to get back to the bus station to go back to Tallahassee.

They seemed relieved to have settled this situation amicably. I told them I should be back the next Tuesday and maybe we could get a burger together then. They said they would like that and I quietly thanked them and said goodbye.

I got in John's car and opened all the windows. Going back down the dusty road, I started thinking about how surreal this whole situation was. I felt like I was in a foreign country, speaking a foreign language and dealing with social morals so different from how I was brought up.

I brought John his car and what I thought was good news. He had seen a lot more of life in Marianna, however, than I had and was somewhat more skeptical than I about the outlook for his case. He thanked me though, and offered to take me to the bus station. On the way he suggested that we stop at his church.

We stopped outside a nice-looking, medium-sized church. We could hear a choir singing as we approached. As we entered we noticed on the stage a group of some 20 Negro kids singing a psalm. They were led by a white girl with long hair down past her waist. Her back was toward us. We sat down and listened for a while.

Their voices sang in unison, softly, then rising to a crescendo. It was a nice reprieve from the tension of the day. After a while, the girl suggested they take a break. She turned to face us and smiled. She walked toward us.

We were both conscious, she and I, that we were the only white people in the church. She offered her hand and we shook. She knew John and greeted him as well. She was incredibly beautiful, almost angelic. Her long, light brown hair hung naturally over her shoulders. Her brown eyes were large and bright. Her smile was happy and left me literally dumbstruck.

She asked what I was doing in Marianna. I gave her a brief summary. She looked sadly at John. I assured her everything was going to work out just fine.

John excused himself and she sat down to talk. She was from Ohio, a student at Oberlin, majoring in music. She would be here for another two months. I told her I would be in Tallahassee for a similar amount of time. We had a connection and we promised to get together. I told her I should be back next Tuesday. She asked me to come by. I said I would.

When I left the church, I was speechless. John had a special grin on his face as he took me to the bus station. I thanked him, assured him once again that I was all over his case and would see him next week. We shook hands and I boarded a Greyhound back to Tallahassee.

I wrote notes all the way back. I imagined a cross-examination of Buster, submitting the statements of the sisters to the judge, an immediate dismissal of the case for a lack of evidence.

Then I thought about the girl. She was perfect. What a match! We both went to small, Midwestern colleges with very high academic standards. We were down in cracker country trying to change the world.

This was the beginning of a relationship that was going to be important. I was walking on air.

The next day I reported all of this to John Due. He took it all in and complimented me on a job well done. The weekend passed and on Monday we reviewed that case. He was ready, he said. Then he said he would go alone to the courthouse the next day.

I pleaded with him to let me join him but he was resolute. I did not understand why he wanted to go alone; the reasons he gave were not convincing to me. But after a time working with John Due and gaining a great deal of experience, I understood his motivation.

Racist judges do not appreciate black and white lawyers working together for a defendant. Any sort of integration they find despicable and challenging within their courtroom. Working in conjunction, most especially with the black man leading the defense, creates a hostile environment which increases the likelihood that the judge will not even listen to the defense's arguments. John Due felt his chances were better if he went alone for those reasons.

I never went back to Marianna, I never saw the sisters again, nor John the defendant nor the future love of my life.

John Due got to the courthouse at 10:30 a.m., with plenty of time for the case but found his client distraught in the courtroom. The court had opened at 9:00 a.m. and his was the first case called.

No witnesses were called; the judge had ignored his pleas to wait for his attorney to arrive. The judge, had however, magnanimously lowered the charge to a misdemeanor, found John guilty and suspended any sentence if he acted on good behavior for the next six months.

It was not clear if John would keep his job, as a misdemeanor probably was insufficient for punishment. But it was a grey area.

I was disappointed. I expected a clear victory, a Perry Mason cross-examination of Buster. A total destruction of the baseless charges. What actually happened was a sad reality. We were finessed by the racist system.

When I was in law school I had a Saturday-night ritual. Regardless of what I did that night, either alone or accompanied, I would always get the early edition of the Sunday New York Times at a newsstand on Seventh Avenue and 4th Street, just south of the Riviera Cafe.

One Saturday night in the fall, I got back to my apartment and opened up the front section. Below the middle of the front page was an article reporting that Martin Luther King had been arrested driving in Kentucky.

The article said it was a trumped-up charge. The real reason for his arrest was that he was in the back seat of a car with a white girl. The girl in question was my friend from the church in Marianna.

Dr. Robert Hayling addressing Governor Haydon Burns about the atrocities committed against Negroes in St. Augustine Florida. Seated next to Dr. Hayling is John Due, esq. a civil rights lawyer based in Tallahassee, Florida, for whom the author worked in the summer of 1965. Next to Mr. Due, is Loucille Plummer, an important local civil rights leader, with whom the author stayed while in St. Augustine in July, 1965, Next to Mrs. Plummer is B.J. Johnson, representing SCLC and Dr. Martin Luther King, Jr. (July, 1965) Photo Florida archives

Mrs. Loucille Plummer's home at 177 Twine Street where the author stayed while in St. Augustine, July, 1965. Photo by Marcelo Guanabara

The facade of the Lightner Museum in the building that was the Alcazar Hotel built in 1888 by Henry Flagler. It is open to the public. Photo by Marcelo Guanabara

The magnificent facade of Flagler College, formerly the Hotel Ponce de Leon built by Henry Flagler in1888. Photo by Marcelo Guanabara

Original 68 foot ceiling of the entrance hallway of the Hotel Ponce de Leon created and installed by Louis Tiffany in 1888. This and numerous other stained glass windows in the dining room were the first important works by Tiffany at the beginning of his career. Photo by Marcelo Guanabara

The plaque honoring Andrew Young for the beating he received from white segregationists in June, 1964. Located near the Slave Market, the beating was even more notorious as law enforcement personnel led by Police chief Virgil Stuart looked on as the beating occurred. Photo by Marcelo Guanabara

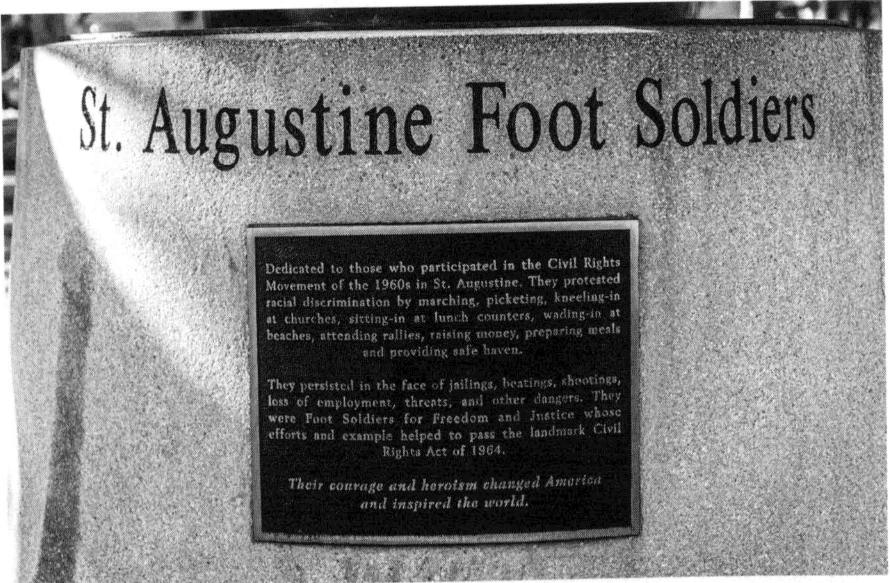

Plaque honoring the civil rights workers that fought against the segregation and discrimination in St. Augustine in the 1960s. The plaque is located near the Slave Market. Photo by Marcelo Guanabara

One of the sculptures near the Slave Market in St. Augustine that honors the soldiers of the civil war and the civil rights workers of the 1960s. Photo by Marcelo Guanabara

The most important structure in St. Augustine: The Slave Market built in the early 1800s in the central square near the water that received ships bringing goods from abroad, it was where all commerce, including the sale of slaves, took place. Photo by Marcelo Guanabara

The Plaque in front of Mrs. Plummer's home at 177 Twine, St. Augustine, Florida. This location, where the author stayed, housed numerous important participants in the civil rights movement of the 1960s. Photo by Marcelo Guanabara

Scene of attempted integration of segregated white beach in St. Augustine in 1964. Photo Florida Archives

The most famous St. Augustine civil rights photo from the 1960s. Dr. King and Ralph Abernathy are refused entrance to Monson's Motor Lodge by its manager, James Brock. June 11, 1964. They were arrested by Police Chief Virgil Stuart for trespassing. This was the only time in all of Dr. King's many arrests that his fingerprints were taken. The cards of these fingerprints are on display at the Lincolnville Musuem and Cultural Center in St. Augustine. Photo Shutterstock

CHAPTER 13

ST. AUGUSTINE, FLORIDA

John Due called me into his office in July 1965. By then I'd had numerous experiences and felt more adapted to an extremely uncomfortable society. I continued to use the "colored" bathrooms when in a gas station or bus station or any other public location. As a result, there were many close calls. In retrospect, I have no idea how I kept calm and continued on. Now I was about to begin my most profound incident while in Florida in the summer of 1965.

A black man in St. Augustine had supposedly hung himself in the St. Johns County jail. John Due had been called to represent the family to investigate the circumstances of his death. The sheriff said it was suicide by hanging and the grand jury agreed. His family and other members of the black community there said he was murdered in the local prison.

"I want you to find out what happened," Mr. Due said to me.

John was a usually happy fellow with a bright outlook on life. He was not smiling. "You have to be very careful there. There has been lots of violence and the local people are crackers of the worst kind. The police will not protect you. If violence starts, they will look away."

He continued, "Mrs. Loucille Plummer will meet you at the bus station. She has offered for you to stay in her house and use her car as needed. She is a wonderful lady; also a very brave leader in the community."

I nodded and the next day I was on a Greyhound east to the city with the Fountain of Youth. At the time, the population of St. Augustine was 15,000, with about 4,000 being Negroes. I knew Dr. King and the SCLC had been there the year before and had a violent reception trying to integrate the local beaches and motels.

The sheriff there had a terrible reputation, having deputized a leader of the Ku Klux Klan and many of his associates. As a result, they were able to batter many Negro demonstrators with impunity.

At the time, Andrew Young, Dr. King's main assistant and future ambassador to the U.N., as well as a future U.S. congressman, said:

"When you have one man, wearing civilian clothes, beating you while another, wearing a badge, stands waiting to arrest you when the first one gets tired, well, that makes you think St. Augustine is really worse than Birmingham. It's the worst I've ever seen."

Understanding the history of the city of St. Augustine will offer additional clarification of the immensity of the effect the civil rights movement had upon it.

Ponce de Leon was credited with discovering St. Augustine and its Fountain of Youth. When I was growing up that is what we learned in school and really was all I knew about the town until I visited it. In fact, it was Ponce de Leon, the governor of Puerto Rico, who ventured north in 1513 and named the land La Florida, thereby claiming it for the Spanish Crown.

St. Augustine was officially founded in 1565. There was lots of back and forth between Spain and France until King Philip II authorized Pedro Menendez de Aviles to control the area for the crown and dispatched the French troops. The date of its official founding is important as, 400 years later, 1965, there would be a quadricentennial celebrating the founding of the city.

Various countries juggled for control over Florida during the early centuries but the Spanish rule dominated and the architecture and spirit of the town and the area around the St. Johns River is clearly Spanish. In 1819, Florida was ceded to the United States.

Union troops took control of St. Augustine in the early 1860s due to the importance of its ports. The fear was that the Confederacy could purchase arms from Europe and receive the shipments in the town's ports. There were many battles in the area during the Civil War and in 1865, Florida rejoined the Union.

A group of freedmen, former slaves liberated by decree after the end of the Civil War, settled in a section of St. Augustine. Initially the area was called "Little Africa" but after the Emancipation Proclamation, the name was changed to Lincolnville.

Lincolnville was characterized by the most beautiful Victorian homes, many of which still exist today. A number of well-known writers owned homes here. This area became a friction point for racial issues and was a center of civil rights demonstrations in the 1960s.

The 1880s saw the arrival of Henry Flagler, who would transform St. Augustine and ultimately all of southeastern Florida into a tourist mecca. Flagler was a partner of John D. Rockefeller in Standard Oil and in the railroads that spread across the country.

Fabulously rich, Flagler built the Hotel Ponce de Leon, a lavish, huge and modern location for the northern elite to spend their winters. He also brought the railroad from the north as far south as St. Augustine.

The town began to boom with these and other investments in the area. Subsequently, Flagler extended the railroad to points south like Palm Beach, Miami and ultimately, Key West. This became the Florida East Coast Railway and was headquartered in St. Augustine.

In my opinion, The Ponce, as it was called, is the story and symbol of the rise and fall of St. Augustine as an important center, principally for tourism, and then a fractured town due to its uncompromising stance against social progress and unfaltering in favor of maintaining segregation.

The Ponce in 1965 was a statuesque, still fabulous five star-hotel; a most impressive and highly sophisticated structure with magnificent Spanish colonial architecture and dramatic landscaping, with 540 rooms and multiple restaurants.

In 1964, The Ponce staunchly opposed any type of integration on its grounds, whether in the use of its rooms or even of its dining areas. Martin Luther King, Jr. and Dr. Robert Hayling made various attempts to use the facilities and were repulsed each time. Below I will relate its fascinating history and its sad demise, along with the equally sad demise of St. Augustine as an important tourist center.

The Ponce was opened in 1888 and represented Flagler's intention to make St. Augustine a southern version of Newport, Rhode Island, even today a posh ocean resort for the rich seeking exclusive accommodations for their families and their yachts.

It was the first hotel to be constructed of poured concrete. It was also the first hotel to have wired electricity throughout its structure. Furthermore, the electrical project was designed and installed under the supervision of Thomas Edison himself! Flagler's vision for St. Augustine anticipated tourism on all levels and he built multiple hotels and other projects, including a mansion for his family residence.

The hotel was built on a former orange grove and quickly became the social center of town, occupying an entire city block. The project was the first for the firm of Carriere and Hastings, whose next project was the New York Public Library in Manhattan. The interior of the hotel was created by Louis Comfort Tiffany and his stained glass windows and Tiffany lamps would be a hallmark of the hotel's distinction. There were murals in the rotunda and the dining room.

At that time, Tiffany was not well known. It was here that he developed his now famous aqua blue coloring for his packaging. Different shades of aqua blue were used in his designs in The Ponce and remain there until today. His stained-glass windows and other stained-glass decoration that remain until today have been evaluated at $100 million.

The Edison Electric Company installed the DC dynamos that powered the hotel. When it opened, Flagler hired staff to turn power on and off for the residents who were afraid of being electrocuted. This staff was much like today's room-service people and were available around the clock for the sole function of turning electricity on and off and on again in each room.

Flagler's friends and acquaintances would come south on his railroad and check into The Ponce in the first week of January and stay for three months. The basic bill for the large rooms would be, in today's currency, around $100,000 for the three-month stay and would be paid in cash upon their arrival. Flagler, by extending his railroad to St. Augustine, enabled his guests to have a non-stop ride from New York to his hotel. He had buggies waiting at the St. Augustine railroad station to carry his guests to his hotel, as well as the luggage for their stay.

These hotel guests could use the facilities of the other Flagler hotels that had areas for sports and other activities. However, the guests in the other hotels could not use the facilities of The Ponce. Its enormous dining room had partially gold-plated ceilings, much of which was painted Tiffany aqua blue which even today is featured on Tiffany boxes, and multiple crystal chandeliers.

Each night, Flagler would sit at the far side of the dining room after his guests were seated. The most important guests were seated close to his table and, with decreasing importance, the remainder of the guests would be seated until the many hundreds filled the room. When Flagler began eating the dinner could begin, but not until then!

Within less than two years, Flagler had fully opened The Alcazar across the street for the guests The Ponce could not accommodate, at a more accessible price point. It housed spas, tennis courts, a bowling alley and the largest indoor pool in the world at the time.

When its original owner could not maintain it, he also purchased a hotel that would be named The Cordova. Additionally, he donated land for the Ancient City Baptist Church and gave money to restore the Catholic church that had been damaged by fire in 1887.

He built a mansion for himself and next door he built the Memorial Methodist Church, whose mausoleum today holds Flagler's remains, as well as that of his first wife and their day-old baby girl.

With the success of his St. Augustine venture, Flagler continued down the coast, building first The Royal Poinciana Hotel in Palm Beach. A wooden structure, it became the largest hotel in the world at the time, with 1,000 rooms and a dining room that could seat 1,600 people.

As if that were not enough, he built an ancillary hotel on the beach which became The Breakers and, like The Ponce, was made of poured cement. That was prescient, as The Royal Poinciana was severely damaged by a horrendous hurricane and subsequently destroyed by a fire. The company opted for expanding the hotel on the beach, which is now a beautiful, historic building, truly a five-star hotel and club. His vision was truly unprecedented, not only then, but also in present-day terms.

He envisioned these Florida locations to be the basis for what he hoped would become the American Riviera.

As Flagler expanded his empire south, aided by expansion of the South Florida Railroad, the warmer locations in Palm Beach and Miami took away part of the northern tourism from St. Augustine. Eventually he extended the railroad all the way to Key West, the most southern point in Florida. When he inaugurated the Key West extension he was 82. However, The Ponce continued to retain its glory right up to the mid-1960s.

CHAPTER 14

THE CIVIL RIGHTS MOVEMENT IN ST. AUGUSTINE

On March 31, 1964, more than a hundred students staged a sit-in in the main dining room of The Ponce. Police with cattle rods and German shepherds removed them and the leaders were arrested. Due to the national attention this demonstration received, it was considered the beginning of the St. Augustine's civil rights movement. However, in fact, the movement had begun in earnest in 1963.

I was to discover that St. Augustine was indeed a microcosm of the worst of the segregated South of our country. It was as bad as Mississippi and Alabama, with the sheriffs and city leaders strident against any changes in favor of equality for blacks, no matter how small.

The local civil rights leaders totally rejected Dr. King's mantra of passive resistance. Dr. Robert Hayling was a local dentist who met with Dr. King and went with him to Washington to lobby President Lyndon Johnson to pass the Voting Rights Act of 1964. He was incredibly brave and inspirational.

But he was openly armed and was quoted as saying that he would "shoot any cracker" who threatened him or anyone in his community. Dr. Hayling denied having said this but the alleged quote stuck and became a point of irritation for the segregationist mayor, Dr. Joseph Shelley, and his supporting cast.

Dr. Hayling moved to St. Augustine in 1960 to take over the dentistry practice of a retiring dentist who had passed away shortly before his arrival there. He was brought up in Tallahassee in a middle-class family. His father was a professor at Florida A&M, from which he and his siblings graduated. This was the "separate but equal" Negro college in Tallahassee. He attended Meharry Medical College School of Dentistry in Nashville, Tennessee, which was also a segregated Negro school. His first contact with overt discrimination came when he entered the Air Force.

Upon establishing himself in St. Augustine, he was shocked with its racism. He spent the next few years building up his dental practice, which flourished. Oddly, the majority of his clients were white, and many were Klan members.

He apparently never had any issues in his practice with regard to race. However, the segregation and lack of public facilities for Negroes ate at him. Additionally, the medical community of St. Augustine would not accept him, not only because of his race but also because he was not native to the city. He was accepted as the first Negro member of The Florida Dental Association but he was never accepted by the local doctors.

Dr. Hayling joined the NAACP, which was then very conservative in general and in St. Augustine, it was virtually silent. Its philosophy was to persuade on a personal one-to-one basis rather than challenge the establishment on a group-to-group basis. With the entrance of Dr. Hayling this would change.

As events in Selma, Birmingham, and other southern cities raged on, it became impossible to ignore local discrimination. Until 1963 he was respected as a quiet, dependable dentist. However, inside he was boiling at the racism and mistreatment of the Negro residents. On a personal basis, he was annoyed at the total ostracism of the medical community.

In early 1963, Dr. Hayling and other NAACP local members asked for a permit to demonstrate against the rampant segregation. The permit was denied without any explanation.

The then-vice president, Lyndon Johnson, was scheduled to come to St. Augustine to dedicate a historical Spanish landmark. Dr. Hayling pressured the NAACP to lobby Johnson to cancel this visit, as Negroes were not included in the events sponsored by the city for this dedication.

In March, Johnson informed the city that he would not be coming if the event were to be segregated. The city formed a small group of local Negroes to participate in the event, led by the president of the local Negro college but excluding anyone from the NAACP.

However, with this first public clash, the die was cast. Dr. Hayling was determined to lead a movement to change St. Augustine's segregationist policies. He wanted jobs in the local government for Negroes, public facilities to be made available to Negroes and segregation in general to be ended. City leaders were averse to changes of any kind to the segregated city.

The creation of a sub-committee made up of carefully chosen Negroes was a ploy that many segregation-prone municipalities used to show they were integrated. This group had absolutely nothing to say in the planning and execution of the ceremonies. They were invisible in every respect. But their nominal presence allowed the city to say the planning committees and other parts of the local organization were integrated. That satisfied the vice president and he attended the celebration.

Another example of such a policy was the "integration" of the state universities. Florida State University (FSU), the largest public university in Florida, is located in Tallahassee. It was considered to be totally segregated with Negroes getting their "equal" education at Florida A&M.

I have previously mentioned the use of token integration in the South but it is especially important to reiterate here.

However, for the record, a Negro student, one Negro student, was admitted in 1961. He did not participate in any student activities and only attended classes. He never went to the student union, never had a Coke on campus and did not use the lavatories or other facilities of the school.

Yet, the university could say it was not segregated!! No Negro leader was aware of his admission and there were no articles about him in the newspapers. While I was living in Tallahassee, no one I knew ever mentioned that there was a Negro amongst the student body. FSU was considered to be an all-white state university and in reality, it really was all white.

After the vice president's visit, Dr. Hayling increased the pressure to desegregate and led a meeting with city officers to discuss the situation. He was met with denials that there was any discrimination in the city. Dr. Hayling listed some of the issues that needed to be addressed and a second meeting was scheduled.

Between the two meetings, however, three incidents became public. The first was a letter from the national NAACP stating that the city had numerous signs indicating areas of segregation and that said signs were illegal. It was warned that failure to take steps to integrate could result in "an ugly Birmingham and a total collapse for the economy and tourism business."

The second issue was the publication of a letter in the local newspaper from the national NAACP calling for a cessation of federal funds to the city for the celebration of the city's quadricentennial.

Lastly, and perhaps most profoundly, Dr. Hayling was quoted in various newspapers with saying that passive resistance "was no good in the face of violence." He also was quoted as saying that the Negro community had "armed ourselves and we will shoot first and ask questions later."

Again, he denied making these statements. Regardless, this is the message that was attached to him at the time.

Dr. Hayling was physically impressive, as well as having an inspirational air.

At a few inches over six feet, with broad shoulders and a deep voice, he commanded respect and if he were your opponent, fear. To me, his approach seemed respectful and firm.

However, to the racist community he presented a threat, both in his desire to eliminate segregation as well as his physical presence. All of the stereotypical racist claims about Negro men at the time were aroused by Dr. Hayling's mien. Hence, the quotes attributed to him about Negroes arming themselves took on extra meaning within the town's power structure.

The white community and local businessmen were infuriated with these statements. The second meeting to address the situation was deemed unsatisfactory by both sides. The commissioners stated there was no segregation, which was patently false, and the Negro side was angered by this stand and the failure to set up a biracial commission to address these issues.

Throughout the battle for civil rights, local and national leaders urged the mayor and other leaders of the community to form a biracial committee to search for common ground and to discuss the racial issues in the community of St. Augustine.

Led by Mayor Shelly, each and every attempt was denied. Dr. Hayling never achieved the formation of a committee. As we will see in 1964 after months of racial strife, with great fanfare, the governor of Florida announced that a biracial committee had been formed in St. Augustine to attempt to achieve racial order in the town. Mayor Shelly, however, in fact, had never agreed to doing that and prevented it from ever happening.

Dr. Hayling stated that 'as of this date' (June 1963), there would be public demonstrations. On June 21, Negroes began canvassing public facilities to see if they employed Negroes and if they allowed Negroes to patronize the locations. On June 25, led by Negro teenagers, demonstrations began in earnest. Sit-ins occurred in Woolworth's, McCrory's and Service Drugs. The lunch counters in each were immediately closed until the demonstrators were removed.

These events, plus Dr. Hayling's perceived remarks, served to make the city leaders and businessmen dig in against any form of desegregation. Additionally, more moderate Negro leaders were now ignored, although it is highly questionable whether this in fact was a change.

The Mayor, Dr.Joseph Shelly, who was also a leading doctor in town and the head of Flagler Hospital, made his resistance clear and got the town commission to join him in opposing any compromise. The mayor and many other leaders attributed this new movement to communist infiltration. The John Birch Society became more important and was led by another leading doctor in the community. Demonstrations grew in frequency and in the number of people demonstrating. Students from the Negro college, Florida Memorial, began joining the demonstrations.

In July, these events continued to grow. The situation became more tense than ever before. Students from both the Negro high school and the Negro college joined in the demonstrations. Sometimes the peaceful demonstrators were attacked by white men and the business owners would call the police advising that the demonstrators were trying to integrate. When the police arrived the demonstrators would have already dispersed.

On July 18, a sit-in at a local pharmacy resulted in the arrests of 16 students. Of this group, seven were juveniles. The "reason" for the arrests was the failure of the students to leave the premises when the police arrived. They were brought before Judge Charles Mathis, Jr. who ordered the "delinquent children" to spend the night in jail. The judge ordered the police to advise the parents to not allow their underage children to attend these demonstrations in the future as the danger of violence was very great.

No charges, however, were filed against any of the demonstrators but Judge Mathis felt he could imprison some of the demonstrators without cause and he did.

On July 23, he let the parents of the children know that they would only be released if the parents promised to keep them from joining future demonstrations. Mathis opposed these demonstrations as he felt they were communist inspired. The parents of four of the children did not agree to the judge's requirement

The next day over 100 students demonstrated at the jailhouse in protest of the judge's decision, which resulted in violent interaction with the police. Sheriff L.O. Davis described the incidents as worse than Birmingham. The police met the demonstrators with nightsticks and there were numerous shoving matches. The police seized a camera of a photographer who was recording the incidents. (I am grateful to David Colburn's book on Racial Change and Community Crisis for his detailed description of these events.)

What happened next clearly illustrates the racism that dominated the thinking of the police and the judiciary in regard to potential change to segregation in St. Augustine.

The four children whose parents did not agree to forbid them from future demonstrations were punished. Judge Mathis transferred the two juvenile boys to the notorious reform school then known as the Florida

School for Boys in Marianna, Florida. The two girls were transferred to Ocala Correctional School.

Officials at both prisons voiced their hesitation to take children who had only warnings against them into a population of hardened, convicted criminals who had committed violent crimes. In fact, as previously mentioned, Judge Mathis sent these young teenagers to these notorious prisons without even charging them with a crime. Even the attorney general of Florida asked Judge Mathis to reconsider.

Judge Mathis declared that he would not let the kids go and was quoted as saying "you cannot do business with those darkies." County officials supported Judge Mathis' decisions and the county attorney congratulated him on his actions.

When the above decisions became known to the public, there was great confusion. The parents were ready to promise that their children would not participate in future demonstrations but the judge said it was out of his hands as custody was now with the prisons that housed them.

In fact, the children had not been accused of any crime so the state attorney declared it was not under his jurisdiction. A state court upheld his interpretation.

An uproar became national as the NAACP demanded the release of the children. Finally, Governor Bryant, after lengthy discussions with his cabinet, signed a release from the state institutions but the order of Judge Mathis that they were delinquent and could not participate in future demonstrations was left standing.

This and many other incidents during the summer of 1963 created a standstill between the Negro community and the white structure of businessmen, doctors and government officials, including county and city police.

Many Negroes lost their jobs: car salesmen, school bus drivers, nurses, inter alia. The Fairchild Corporation called a meeting of Negro workers and warned them if they demonstrated they would be fired. Maids, waiters and wives of male demonstrators were warned to stay out of the demonstrations.

Sheriff Davis advised companies when their Negro employees were involved in demonstrations. When he arrested them, he publicized their home addresses. Frequently, this information led to violence against their homes.

Governor Bryant was outspoken in his opposition to the demonstrations. He felt it was natural that a motel owner or restaurant manager could choose who to serve and who not to serve. The local John Birch Society became ever more active and brought in speakers on a weekly basis to oppose any changes.

Meanwhile, the demonstrations became larger and more frequent. The white leaders continued to blame communist influence on motivating the movement.

Sheriff Davis vocally accused all sympathizers of being communists. He and others felt resisting integration was the same as guaranteeing the 'American Way.' Mayor Shelly allowed a few Negro students into some schools to illustrate that there was no segregation. However, he limited the numbers to single digits so true integration did not happen in any city institution.

Tension increased as the number of demonstrators increased. Sit-ins and lie-ins occurred all over the city. Although dominated by students in great numbers, older people began to join in.

On the other side, the police acquired dogs and cattle prods. They started to demand permits for the demonstrations. Many leaders were charged with resisting arrest and sentenced to prison terms. Police violence, which was rare in previous years, became common in 1963. The police chief openly sided with the John Birch Society. Almost anything was justified in the face of the "advancing communist threat."

Sheriff Davis was the most powerful person in the city and the county. He became more fearful of the alleged communist threat posed by these demonstrations. This perception, without any basis in fact, was convenient for the local authorities.

Everyone hated communists but many people were sympathetic to the movement that clamored for change. By alleging that anyone demonstrating for racial equality was a communist, the segregationist power could avoid facing the question of racial discrimination head on.

The response of "We have to prevent the communists from ruining our community" would attempt to mobilize opposition to the civil rights movement without discussing the merits of the civil rights movement.

With the rise of more violence, the KKK became more active. As the national NAACP began citing the clashes in St. Augustine, the city became part of the national scene for both the Negro side, if you will, as well as the side of those resisting any change.

White supremacist leaders began coming to the city to incite the white community to resist. September saw more violence and more activity by both sides of the issue. And more national attention to the events in this Florida tourist town caused further tension. It should be remembered that all of these demonstrations were carried out by local people. During 1963, there were virtually no demonstrators as yet coming from the North.

The tension reached a crescendo in September with a large KKK rally being called.

The "Reverend" Connie Lynch arrived from California with his pink Cadillac and racist speeches. He helped call for a rally on the northern edge of St. Augustine.

An enormous cross was erected near US 1. A crowd of some 300 people gathered. The cross was set on fire and robed Klansmen and women walked in a circle around the burning cross.

Lynch spoke to the crowd saying the recent killing of four young girls at a Negro church in Birmingham was not sad as the press tried to convey. "If there are four less niggers tonight we are all better off."

The crowd became riled up with his speech and started shouting "Nigger, Nigger, Nigger" as Lynch specifically cited Dr. Hayling as a "burr-headed bastard of a dentist." He screamed at the crowd that if they were real men, "half the men you claim to be, you would kill him before the sun rises."

Dr. Hayling had seen the pamphlets calling for **a** KKK meeting and was concerned as to the plans the group might be making. He and three other black men went to the outskirts of the meeting to listen.

However, the Klan had lookouts surrounding the meeting and one saw the four black men. (These events were described to me in November 2018 by Mr. James "Jimmy" Jackson, one of the men with Dr. Hayling that night.) Quickly, the men were surrounded and beaten badly. Dr. Hayling described the event as follows:

"After being beaten severely, we were stacked like cordwood on top of each other .... One of the leaders had asked the people assembled if they had ever had the pleasure of smelling a nigger burn."

Mr. Jackson told me that he remembers after being beaten badly, the Klansmen debated what to do with the bodies. "First, they suggested death by burning. Another said he preferred hanging," he said. "When a third suggested castration, I turned and took off but was grabbed again."

Before the four men could be killed, Sheriff Davis intervened. In fact, according to Mr. Jackson, the sheriff was already at the gathering. A member of the Florida Human Relations Committee had officially advised the sheriff's office, as well as the FBI and the governor's office, that the murders were imminent. It is questionable if the sheriff would have intervened, but when an official advisory was made, he was forced to act.

Davis arrested four Klansmen who were huddled over the four Negroes. He took the four Negroes to the segregated Flagler Hospital with broken bones, deep scalp wounds and multiple abrasions. Rarely were blacks treated at the segregated hospital but exceptions were made in the emergency room when the seriousness of the case required immediate attention.

A jury trial followed and the Klansmen were released, as Dr. Hayling and the others could not identify their attackers. Although Sheriff Davis witnessed the entire scene he did not testify as to who beat the four black men.

An all-white jury of six, however, found Dr. Hayling guilty of assault as it was described by two Klansmen. The judge was less convinced of his guilt and fined him only $100 with no jail time.

The fact that Sheriff Davis was not called as a witness in the trial of the white men who attacked Dr. Hayling's group is one more egregious illustration of how pervasive racism was throughout the justice system.

He arrested these men, for which they went on trial. Who could better describe what happened and why they were arrested than the arresting officer?

However, if these men were convicted of assault against Negroes, especially against Dr. Hayling, St. Augustine's most prominent civil rights activist, there would be a social uproar and Sheriff Davis would be the focal point of it all. To avoid that, justice was again undone and racism was triumphant.

Dr. Hayling's bravery over the following years was heroic and his meetings and demonstrations in St. Augustine with Dr. King and other leaders were credited with accelerating the process, causing President Johnson to enact the Voting Rights Act of 1964 much sooner than he had planned.

Reflecting on the events of 1964, Harper's Magazine had this to say in its January 1965 edition:

"After months of racial disorder, St. Augustine today is an exhausted little town, with worn-out people and a crippled economy; moreover, it is perhaps the most bitterly divided community in the North American continent ....The city's institutions of law and order have cracked under the strain ..... and its Negro community .... is both wounded and determined."

Dr. Hayling had been frustrated by the NAACP's go-slow approach and approached Dr. King to join his attempts to further integration in St. Augustine. While Dr. King had not come to St. Augustine himself, he had sent representatives to meet with Dr. Hayling and work out a strategy on how his SCLC could have maximum impact to further integration. Although hesitant at first, in May of 1964 he and the directors of SCLC determined that St. Augustine would become a center of activity for their organization.

Their focus took into consideration the importance of tourism to the country's oldest city and the fact that in 1965 it would have a 400-year celebration of its founding. The city intended that the president would attend and that the country would join in the celebration.

Dr. Hayling would use this celebration as a cornerstone to protest the city's segregationist policies and its refusal to obey the Brown decision requiring the end of segregation in government facilities.

In the spring, having been informed of Dr. King's intention to come to the city, he put out a call to college students in the North to use their Easter/Spring break and summer vacations to come to St. Augustine and help attain voter registration and further the movement for integration. He also lobbied President Johnson to not attend the 1965 quadricentennial celebration if blacks were not included in the planning and execution of the festivities.

On May 18, 1964, Dr. King formally made public SCLC's intention to come to St. Augustine to help attain integration. His representatives tried to meet with the city leaders with no success. The mayor considered them to be outside agitators, communist inspired, with the intention of trying to destroy the fabric of the town's traditions. Dr. King wrote Attorney General Robert Kennedy as follows: "The situation in St. Augustine highlights the need for the protection of minorities provided by the Civil Rights Bill."

He urged the attorney general to use federal troops to halt the violence and brutality against black residents.

SCLC leaders, headed by Hosea Williams, came to St. Augustine to orient those interested in joining the demonstration as to how to act within the principles of non-violence and how to comport themselves so as not to give any stimulus to mob violence.

These activities brought to light the divisions in the black community. The young blacks were anxious to be part of the movement and attended all of Williams' meetings.

The older blacks did not. Some had already lost jobs because relatives had participated in the demonstrations of 1963. Others were fearful more people would lose their jobs. They had lived for decades under rigid segregation and knew the powers that be in the city would not tolerate any change.

They also felt that SCLC would stay for awhile and then leave, resulting in the local community being left alone to deal with the violence of the white community. These fears were justified.

The mayor, sheriff, town council and other authorities, including judges, made clear their opposition to any change, no matter how small, and made clear their unwillingness to even meet with anyone advocating integration of any sort.

The lines had been drawn. As the SCLC declared they would be coming to St. Augustine to desegregate the city, the Klan advocated violence and numerous members of the white majority joined them in threatening the black citizens.

Many shootings and other forms of violence occurred and the situation had become electric. Mayor Shelley made various declarations to verbally attempt to keep the peace; however, he condemned the demonstrations of the black citizens and accused Dr. King and his supporters of being communists. As he and other leaders refused any meetings, and began to take a lower profile, the racist leaders began to be quoted in the papers and on TV as representing the local community.

The town's police chief, Virgil Stuart, had never restrained any attacks against blacks because they were "communists trying to change our values and our society."

Many of the town's deputies were Klansmen and KKK sympathizers. A grand jury investigated the reasons for the rampages and concluded that Dr. Hayling's public statements and overt demonstrations were its cause. This conclusion was quickly used by the authorities and by the Klan's population as a justification for repression of the demonstrations.

Sheriff Davis, who early on had been seen as less radical, declared that he was convinced that Dr. King was a communist and would undermine St. Augustine's values if left unchecked.

His brother operated a family store on Washington Street in the heart of Lincolnville. The black residents frequented this store and he wanted to protect his brother's business. As tensions escalated, Sheriff Davis also became more radicalized against desegregation.

Hoss Manucy was a Klan leader and very violent. In the fall of 1963 he was driving through Lincolnville threatening to kill any blacks he saw. When he passed through Palm Street, shots were fired at the car striking his partner, William Kincaid, killing him instantly.

Manucy alleged they were returning from hunting but the only shots fired from their guns was from Kincaid's shotgun, which resulted from his being shot. This killing exacerbated an already tense situation and the echoes continued throughout the first semester of 1965.

Manucy had a hunting club in St. Augustine that served as the unofficial headquarters of the Klan. After Kincaid's funeral, the Klan held a closed meeting where he and Reverend Connie Lynch spoke.

Later that evening, Harlem Gardens, a local black hangout that had various bars inside and outside, with dance music, was shot at multiple times. A hand grenade was thrown on the roof but did not explode.

Sheriff Davis went to the black hangout and arrested Dr. Hayling that night for "hindering the investigation" of Kincaid's death. This type of interaction continued for the next six months when in May, Dr. King made his declaration that he was targeting St. Augustine as a racist town that resisted any type of desegregation and required the SCLC to try to remedy the situation.

The black community was not united. After the grand jury's declaration that Dr. Hayling was at fault, Roy Wilkins, president of the NAACP, supposedly told Hayling to resign or he would close the St. Augustine chapter. Both Dr. Hayling and Reverend Goldie Ewbanks resigned. (All of the above facts were taken from numerous FBI reports, among other sources.)

In January, 1964, shootings by the Manucy-led Klan began again in earnest. Shots were fired into the residence of Dr. Hayling, killing his dog but not harming his family. Dr. Hayling was in his dentist's office, unaware of the incident.

Various black citizens were beaten without any cause. National attention returned to St. Augustine. The mayor, sheriff and the editor of the St. Augustine Record called for calm and to an end of the barbarity. The local economy was in decline and the attention to the renewed violence would only serve to inhibit tourism even more.

A federal judge, Bryan Simpson, became the appeal of last resort. Judge Simpson ordered Sheriff Davis to remove deputies who were associated with the Klan, most specifically Hoss Manucy and his followers, who openly abused black citizens and violently repressed peaceful demonstrations by black (mostly young students) citizens.

Dr. King was campaigning for unprecedented civil rights legislation and a new voting-rights law. He felt an additional front outside of Alabama was necessary and the entreaties of Dr. Hayling caused him, after in-depth analysis of St. Augustine's unsuccessful attempts to desegregate, to eventually determine that it should be the new focus in 1964.

Hosea Williams, Dr. King's principal assistant, came to the city with a sophisticated plan to organize local citizens to mobilize in favor of change to its segregated society. Additionally, as did Dr. Hayling previously, he exhorted northern students to come to St. Augustine during Easter break and summer vacation to join the movement.

Mrs. Endicott Peabody, the 72 year-old mother of the then-governor of Massachusetts, and the wife of a well-known Episcopal minister in the same state, announced she would be coming to St. Augustine to join the demonstrations.

Mayor Shelley responded to a question about his thoughts of her impending trip by saying, "If she comes down and breaks the law, she will be arrested."

And that is exactly what happened. All of the major American newspapers reported about the arrest and her jail time. She attempted to have dinner at a motel on the edge of town with a group of her friends, which included some black people. She was immediately taken to jail and put in a cell with six white friends.

The New York Times reported her comments. "There are seven of us in one cell, all white women, and we have running water and a shower."

Sheriff Davis had met them at the hotel and escorted them to the county jail, where the women refused to post bail.

Prior to the arrest, Mrs. Peabody went to the local Episcopal church for Sunday services, only to find that the rector had cancelled the service so as to avoid conflict and desegregation.

Simultaneously, Hosea Williams organized some 300 youths to march to the Slave Market. As the name indicates, this location had once been used to buy and sell slaves much as horses were sold.

According to the New York Times, the march was peaceful and when they were all together at the market's park, "they sang several freedom songs." Nearby, a group of elderly white men played their daily card games, unbothered by the demonstration.

Shortly thereafter, about 150 of the group walked over to the nearby Ponce Hotel and sat down in the dining room at the elaborately laid-out dining tables with white tablecloths, silver and glassware. It wasn't long before the police came to arrest the marchers but they objected and walked away from them and their German shepherds, with no attempt by the officers to restrain them.

Many consider Mrs. Peabody's arrest as a watershed moment for the city as national attention was suddenly focused on its continued resistance to integration. The local leaders characterized Mrs. Peabody's presence as an invasion and justified her arrest as a natural response to the invasion.

In response to the Easter activity, the local segregationist leaders also had Mrs. Loucille Plummer and the local SCLC treasurer fired from their jobs. Mrs. Peabody was a guest at Mrs. Plummer's house and stayed in the same room that I subsequently stayed in in 1965.

Five other demonstrators were also fired from their jobs. Mrs. Plummer had been a nurse at Flagler Hospital, where the mayor was president of the board and a principal physician. He had been previously warned that her civil rights activities, if continued, could result in her dismissal and that weekend was the final straw. She was an important civil rights leader for many years and accompanied Dr. Hayling to important events in favor of civil rights.

White doctors also informed their Negro patients that they were raising what they charged them for office visits as of this date. The president of Florida Memorial College warned students that they would be suspended if they continued to demonstrate. He did this after threats to withhold local funding for the college if he refused to make the warning.

Judge Mathis refused to accept bonds for the arrested demonstrators by a Daytona bondsman after local bondsmen refused to post bond. Additionally, Sheriff Davis would not accept checks from those arrested to post bond and he also tripled the bonds for those arrested.

SCLC lawyers appealed these actions to Judge Bryan Simpson who rejected the appeal. This rejection, plus the return of the northern demonstrators to their homes, encouraged local leaders to maintain their no-holds-barred attitude in resisting change.

However, the campaign continued as Mrs. Peabody appeared on the Today Show on NBC and characterized the situation in St. Augustine as violent and dangerous. Letters to the New York Times emphasized the local resistance to any type of desegregation and called on the federal government to not support the upcoming celebrations of the 400th anniversary of the country's oldest city.

Mayor Shelley demanded equal time on the Today Show. Finally on May 19, he was interviewed by Ray Shearer, an important correspondent for NBC news, along with the head of the quadricentennial observance. They refused to concede there was any discrimination in St. Augustine, insisting there was total peace between the races.

For his version, Mayor Shelley emphasized that despite major steps having been taken to establish racial equality, Dr. Hayling and other leaders had done "irreparable harm" to the advances being made. He also charged that Mrs. Peabody "Did a disservice not only to St. Augustine but the nation as a whole."

St. Augustine and St. Johns County re-elected Sheriff Davis with 70% of the vote in May 1964. As he had gained national attention as an unrelenting opponent of integration, as notorious as the sheriffs in Alabama and Georgia, this result was taken as strong support for resisting integration in the area.

In fact, Sheriff Davis' attitude toward the Negro population had hardened with the continued demonstrations for equal rights to the point that he actually went into the Lincolnville area to tell residents to not vote for him.

Using the overt language of "nigra" and other pejorative names, he tried to demonstrate his pro-segregationist views clearly and loudly. Prior to the election, he allowed the notorious Klan leader Manucy and Klan agitator, J.B. Stoner, complete access to his office.

He told a close friend that if he were not sheriff, he would knock Dr. King's teeth out the next time he showed up in St. Augustine. This friend told multiple people and the sheriff's quote spread throughout the town.

Sheriff Davis made a big show of arresting Mrs. Peabody, thereby getting national attention. He followed this up with regular updates on her condition in the 24 hours she was in jail. While this brought him national notoriety, it brought him full approval of the local population, all of which led to his overwhelming victory in his re-election.

These events were not lost on Dr. King and the SCLC. Their battle to get the civil rights and voting rights bills passed by the Senate needed additional impetus and a new front for demonstrations that could rouse the national interest and garner support for their proposed bills. They concluded that they would return to St. Augustine with full strength to attempt to desegregate public facilities and confront the local powers that be.

In mid-May, Dr. King made a formal announcement of SCLC's return with "a non-violent army." He wrote Attorney General Robert Kennedy that the situation in St. Augustine "highlights the need for the protection of minorities provided by the Civil Rights Bill." (David Colburn, Racial Change and Community Crisis-St. Augustine)

On May 26, Dr. King arrived in St. Augustine and met with 400 people at the First Baptist Church. After an emotional speech by Dr. King, Hosea Williams spoke about the importance of non-violence and asked the group if they wanted to march to the Slave Market.

Greeted with resounding approval, the group organized outside the church and 400 people marched to the downtown market. Surprisingly, there were no white crowds to harass them. The march was peaceful and after singing various songs of the movement, they ended with a rousing version of "We Shall Overcome."

The next evening the scene basically repeated itself. However, a block from the town center the marchers came upon Sheriff Davis and Police Chief Stuart. They informed Hosea Williams that there was a large crowd of white people at the Slave Market and they could not assure the marchers' safety.

After a few minutes, some of the children and older people left the march but about 350 people continued to the main park that contained the slave market. They were met with jeers from a group of white teenagers and some objects were thrown at the marchers. The march concluded, this time without anyone being hurt and without major incidents. But many of the marchers reported that they had seen some armed people in the crowd.

The following evening the events began again and some 400 marchers left the church in the direction of the market. However, this time television crews and reporters were present. As they approached the market, they were met with a much more aggressive crowd. When the lights from the TV crew went on in order to film the events, the crowd violently attacked the camera crews and reporters with clubs, chains and other items.

The local police were unsympathetic to the marchers and stood by watching the assaults and even allowed their dogs to attack the marchers. One of the SCLC leaders got caught in the dog's leash and fell to the ground, with the deputy on top of him throwing punches. When they became untangled, the leader asked the deputy where his camera was and got this reply: "Let Khrushchev buy you another one." (Colburn)

Later shots were fired at one of the SCLC leader's car and Dr. King's rented cottage was struck by gunfire The violence had been raised to an unprecedented level.

Dr. King contacted the U.S. president's office and requested federal protection as the local police were able to control the violence. A presidential assistant, in turn, spoke with Governor Farris Bryant, who assured them all that he was sending guardsmen to control the situation. The president's office made it clear that federal intervention would be inappropriate at this time and insisted the governor would intervene.

Andrew Young and two others met with Mayor Shelley and gave a list of demands which the mayor rejected out of hand. On June 1, the city commission, in response to Sheriff Davis' statement that he could no longer guarantee stability as long as the marches continued, passed an ordinance prohibiting people under the age of 18 to be in the streets between 9 p.m. and 5 a.m.

It also prohibited parking downtown during those hours. As so many of the marchers were teenagers under 18, the mayor and sheriff felt this would end the demonstrations. However, the lawyers for SCLC appealed in federal court against the constitutionality of the ordinance and on June 9, Judge Simpson ruled that the decree violated the marchers' First Amendment rights of free speech and assembly.

The mayor and Sheriff Davis were furious with this decision and refused to meet with SCLC, whose leaders announced that the marches would resume. Repeating the old line of claiming SCLC and the marchers were communists led by outside agitators, the city leaders took a step away from the issues while Klan leaders and other outspoken segregationists came to the forefront.

Hoss Manucy became a leading spokesman against the SCLC and made numerous inflammatory statements condemning the marches. Referring to the almost 1,500 members of his Ancient City Hunting Club, he stated, "We are better organized than the niggers are, and the niggers know it."

He was a stereotypical figure for the segregationists. According to Professor Colburn, "Manucy lived some six miles outside of town in a dilapidated house with his wife and 14 children, a yard full of dogs, a few animals and nothing else."

He usually wore a black cowboy hat and his pot belly hung well over his belt. His statements on race relations echoed the feelings of the poor whites in and around the town. Keeping the blacks down allowed them a certain amount of status despite their own poor living conditions.

The more the press covered the heated situation in St. Augustine, the more Klan leaders and their members were attracted to support the segregationists in repressing the movement led by the SCLC. Manucy bragged that the walkie talkie system he had established was better than that of the police. He added that he could mobilize hundreds of sympathizers in moments.

Sheriff Davis was close to Manucy and his followers. During the summer, a number were made deputies, including Manucy himself. Sheriff Davis left no doubt as to whose side he was on. The FBI reported that Manucy frequently rode with the sheriff in the latter's car.

After Dr. King's house was ransacked and burned on June 8, appeals were again made to President Johnson to intervene. Again the governor was informed and finally he sent highway patrolmen to keep the peace.

However, when Andrew Young led a march downtown of some 350 people, thugs jumped out from behind Trinity Church and beat him and another leader badly. There were deputies standing close by who did nothing to help, alleging their anger at Judge Simpson's ruling caused the disturbance.

The next day Governor Bryant sent 100 more highway patrolmen to try to establish order.

Today there is a tribute to Andrew Young in the park that houses the Slave Market for the beating that he endured.

While the U.S. Senate took important steps toward a vote on the Civil Rights Bill, Dr. King came back to St. Augustine with the expressed intent to integrate restaurants and hotels in the town or get arrested trying.

On June 11, with television reporters and their cameras waiting, Dr. King and his committee approached Monson's Motor Lodge. This location was chosen, as its manager, James Brock, was a prominent hotelier, then serving as the president of the state association.

Brock stood on his red welcome mat in front of his restaurant. In front of a crowd of demonstrators led by Dr. King, Mr. Brock informed him that he was trespassing on private property.

With cameras clicking and lights flashing, Dr. King told Mr. Brock that he would have to integrate. Mr. Brock said he would if he were to be ordered by a court or encouraged to do so by the local business leaders. As they spoke, a local white man pushed through the crowd demanding to be allowed to enter the restaurant, while calling Dr. King a "black bastard."

Shortly, Chief Virgil Stuart arrived and arrested Dr. King and some of his people for trespassing. Dr. King's prints were taken at the city jail and he was incarcerated. (The fingerprint cards are on display today at St. Augustine's Lincolnville Civil Rights Museum.) The president again refused to send help and the governor sent another 50 patrolmen to the town.

The mayor refused the entreaties of some local businesses to meet with SCLC leaders to try to defuse the situation. United States Senator George Smathers blamed the situation on outside agitators and asked SCLC to withdraw to allow local people to settle their differences. All significant local legislators were unanimous in their condemnation of the SCLC.

On the June12, the demonstrators gathered again. But this time a large white group, who had received a parade permit from the city, began a march from the slave market to Lincolnville, led by the notorious Klan leader, J.B. Stoner.

"Tonight we are going to find out if white people have any rights," he said. 'The coons have been parading around ... for a long time."

He again accused Dr. King of being a communist and stated that they wanted to associate with white people because "they are tired of associating with filthy, sorry niggers" Then they headed off to "niggertown." (Prof. Colburn)

There was no assaults that night nor on the following two nights when the segregationists' marches were repeated. Violence had been avoided and the marches by the SCLC groups continued on a daily basis.

It was summertime and the tourists came, but in smaller numbers than normal for this time of year. The business leaders were very concerned but the mayor and his supporters stood firm against any meetings or committees, much less any concessions that were demanded by SCLC.

SCLC took its demonstrations to the segregated beaches, with national attention. There was no violence but large groups of segregationists gathered and shouted obscenities at the demonstrators. The police were able to keep the peace.

On June 18, some black demonstrators jumped into the pool at the Monson Motor Inn. Reporters had been advised and national attention was again focused on the now notorious location. Brock, the owner, not only was under pressure from the blacks trying to integrate, but also from the segregationists who warned him he would be killed if he allowed Negroes in his hotel or restaurant.

When Brock, a religious man, saw the Negroes in his pool, invited by two white people who were staying in his hotel, he ran to his office to retrieve a two-gallon receptacle that he said was acid and dumped it into the pool.

A city police officer ordered the Negroes out of the pool and arrested them. Another officer jumped into the pool and pummeled the whites who had invited the Negroes to swim. Arrests were made and multiple fights broke out led by local officers against those trying to integrate.

National TV stations broadcast tapes of these events and all the major newspapers had photos of the clashes on their front pages. Meanwhile, a grand jury that had been convened a few weeks previously issued a report blaming SCLC for stirring up trouble and asked that all outsiders leave so peace could be restored. The report contended that the situation in St. Augustine was no worse than most cities in the country. Their biggest problem, the report contended, was the invasion of civil rights workers from all over the country.

The grand jury report only served to worsen an already hyper situation. Both sides raised the level and more demonstrations ensued. Frequently the police lost patience and beatings occurred.

Once Sheriff Davis, clearly frustrated, grabbed Hosea Williams, the ostensible SCLC leader when Dr. King was out of town, and with some of his deputies, pummeled Williams viciously. The next day, a wade-in on a major beach almost ended tragically as large groups gathered.

With SCLC continuing to demonstrate daily and hostile meetings of the segregationists, led by Klan leaders who came from all over the South, the situation was explosive. To calm the situation, Governor Bryant decreed that in order to maintain order all demonstrations from both sides would be prohibited. He specifically asked Judge Simpson to not overrule this order so as to prevent violence that appeared to all to be inevitable.

On June 20, Judge Simpson reversed the governor's order and threatened to hold him in contempt if he tried to enforce the prohibition against demonstrations. That same day the Civil Rights Bill was passed.

While Dr. King rejoiced over both decisions, the segregationists were furious and reiterated their opposition to both Judge Simpson's decisions and the new law that had just been passed.

Near the end of June, the beaches became a daily battlefront. On one wade-in led by the Reverend Elizabeth Miller of the American Baptist Convention, a predominantly white organization, resulted in a serious conflict where the reverend was beaten so badly that her nose was broken and she nearly drowned. The local police, as well as the highway patrol sent in by the governor, stood idly by while the violence occurred.

After a month of constant demonstrations and increasing mayhem, the sides became battle weary. The law-enforcement populace were clearly on the side of the segregationists, which helped embolden the white groups toward violence. The situation was extremely explosive and the SCLC, though pleased with passage of the Civil Rights Act, had grown tired of the local intransigence, as well as the savagery toward their demonstrations.

Violence at the beach escalated and night demonstrations from both sides reflected that, with shots and beatings becoming more prevalent. The federal government still refused to interfere. Mayor Shelley refused to form a committee to try to find a solution, which he felt would be perceived to be a victory for Dr. King.

Nevertheless, Governor Bryant announced that both sides had agreed to the creation of a committee, which was clearly untrue. In response to the governor's announcement and weighted down by accelerated expenses, in early July Dr. King announced he would suspend his campaign in the hopes that local people would find a peaceful solution and that public facilities would be desegregated as demanded by the new Civil Rights bill.

The state highway patrolmen left the area, and the local police kept to themselves. The mayor and other leaders kept a low profile. But on July 4, 62 robed Klansmen and an additional 150 people marched through downtown St. Augustine yelling anti-black slogans. The group led by Manucy, Stoner and Lynch held up placards reading, inter alia, "Delicious Food—Eat with Niggers Here," "Niggers Sleep here—Would you?" and "Civil Rights Has To Go."

Many of the businesses, including the Monson Motel, that had desegregated, were facing intense pressure and multiple threats of violence. Within a short period of time, they resegregated as their business sagged. Judge Simpson quickly ordered them to "re-desegregate or face fines of $500-$1000." (Colburn)

In late July, after Brock publicly stated he would respect the Civil Rights Act and allow Negroes to eat at his restaurant, two Molotov cocktails were thrown into the restaurant causing $3,000 in damages. The businessmen were caught in a serious dilemma: Stay segregated and be fined for violating the new law or desegregate and suffer attacks from the segregationists.

Dr. Hayling celebrated the new laws and took credit for the St. Augustine crisis being essential to their rapid passage. Dr. King returned in mid-July to demand desegregation and the governor's support toward maintaining the peace but essentially Dr. King and the SCLC had left

St. Augustine for good. In fact, neither he nor his principal assistants ever returned there.

Furthermore, with SCLC's departure, the press moved to other areas and St. Augustine returned to the background. The sides were still totally separated and the black population felt abandoned, while the segregationists felt emboldened.

A few months passed with few public demonstrations but in January 1965 the new head of the local chapter of the NAACP asked for a closed meeting with the town council to try to set up a committee to discuss the racial situation. She was rebuffed.

The city's Florida Memorial College depended on state and local funding to continue functioning. R.W. Puryear was its president and he had a very difficult job as his student body was stridently in favor of ending the segregation in St. Augustine while the people in charge of the school's funding were firmly against any change in the segregation.

The school had a student exchange program with Bates College in Maine. Bates is a small liberal arts college made of almost exclusively in 1965 of white, well-educated students. During the Easter holidays, a group of Bates students came down to see their sister college. They were all white and were housed in the Negro college.

This was totally unacceptable to the local whites and they were extremely unfriendly to the Bates students and their hosts. One night, the students decided they wanted to have some Kentucky Fried Chicken and went into the restaurant to pick up their dinner.

A crowd gathered outside, acting and yelling in a very threatening manner. Clearly the students could not exit through the front door. As they made their way out the back door they ran to their cars. Some were grabbed and beaten by the segregationist crowd. They returned to the college but were very careful after that not to make waves downtown.

Such was the situation when John Due sent me there in the summer of 1965.

CHAPTER 15

MY TIME IN ST. AUGUSTINE

When the Greyhound pulled into St. Augustine's bus station, Mrs. Plummer greeted me. She thanked me for coming and went into great detail about the case I was to work on.

The deceased's widow received a visit from a county deputy who told her that her husband had committed suicide the previous night in the county jail. She was told his body would be available to be picked up for burial in a few days after the coroner completed his report.

The widow told Mrs. Plummer that she did not believe them. Her husband was not easily upset and was very hardworking. They have two little boys and their father loved them. "He would not have abandoned them," the widow told her.

Mrs. Plummer took many deep breaths and was visibly upset while telling me this story. She made it clear that she did not believe it was a suicide.

"Sheriff Davis is a racist and has been very rough on our community," she told me. "He accuses us of being communists and thinks we want to take over St. Augustine. That is ridiculous."

She went on to give me a brief history of race in St. Augustine. "The two most powerful men in St. Augustine are the mayor and the county sheriff. St. Johns County is much larger than just St. Augustine and Sheriff Davis runs everything in the entire area. There is a city police chief here in town but he follows everything Davis tells him to do.

"Everybody here knows everybody. It is a very small town. People like myself are not popular with the police or the mayor. We live in a community that has been made tense by the movement for civil rights. The whites do not give an inch.

"The pressure to maintain segregation here is fierce," she went on. "But this incident cost the life of an innocent man who did not take kindly to being discriminated against. He did not demonstrate with us. He was not active in trying to change anything. He just did not like to be pushed around, did not like not being able to go where white people went. And he did not believe in non-violence. Somewhere in this mix, he got himself killed. I guess you are here to try and find out how that happened."

Mrs. Plummer drove me to her house in Lincolnville at 177 Twine

Street. She showed me the room I would be using and I left my belongings there, such as they were. We decided I should start at the jail and she offered her car and gave me directions on how to get there.

I drove out of town and went north on U.S.1. Today the road is lined with motels and strip malls. In 1965 there were mostly empty fields alongside the road. I followed a sign toward the county jail, which was atop a slight rise of land.

The reception desk was located at a window that permitted a clear view of all approaching cars. I slowly entered the jail where an officer greeted me quizzically. "How can I help you?" he offered.

"Good afternoon officer," I responded. "I am a legal assistant and would like to see, if possible, where the Negro inmate committed suicide."

The officer looked me over. We were both in our early 20s but could not be more different in background, I imagined.

"Do you have permission from the sheriff," he inquired, poker-faced.

"No, sir." I responded flatly.

The officer picked up the black phone on his desk and dialed a number. "Sheriff, there is a gentleman here who is a lawyer and wants to inspect the cell where the nigger killed himself." He listened intently and then responded, "Yes sir, I understand."

Then again, "Yessa. I will sir."

He hung up and gave a whistle. A German shepherd ran into the room and went right for me. It stopped short in front of me with its nose up against my private parts. I could feel the warm breath from his nose through my jeans. It was very uncomfortable. I immediately broke into a sweat that was similar to when I had played basketball for 20 minutes in 90-degree heat.

"The sheriff says you have 10 seconds to leave here. Then this dog will attack you."

"But officer ..." I began, but was immediately interrupted.

"Nine seconds .... Eight."

"OK, but could you have the dog at least give me some room to move please?"

He gave a command and the dog retreated. I walked toward the door.

"Where can I find the sheriff?" I asked.

He gave me an address and I left. I was soaked in sweat.

In the car, I turned on the motor and took off to go downtown. The wind was blowing through the open windows and gradually I relaxed. The use of German shepherds to repress demonstrations was all over the news, principally in Alabama.

I later learned it was a more recent development in St. Augustine. I was not expecting that type of reception. Until this day, I clearly remember the scary, uncomfortable feeling of the dog's hot breath on my crotch as vividly as if it just happened.

I parked Mrs. Plummer's red and white Plymouth on King Street. Hunger reminded me that I had not eaten yet today so I jumped into the Woolworth five-and-dime store and grabbed two burgers and a Coke. (That same lunch counter has been preserved in its original form at the Wells Fargo branch that took its place on King Street.)

Then I walked over to the sheriff's office. I had not noticed that the only people eating lunch at Woolworth's were white. I would be reminded of that later in the day.

I entered the sheriff's office and asked the officer at the first desk if I could speak with the sheriff. He took my name and the fact that I just came from the county jail where they directed me to come here. I did not offer any further details of the encounter. The officer, after speaking with the sheriff, told me he would see me shortly.

As I looked around the non-descript area, the mood was somewhat sleepy. Before I could get very deep in my observations, a voice called me to come in. It was Sheriff L.O. Davis himself. I arose and followed him into another undecorated office to which he closed the door.

We shook hands. I was taught to look directly in the eyes of the person I was meeting and keep a very firm handshake. I did just that and the sheriff winced a bit.

"Sheriff, I apologize for going to your jail without speaking to you first. I just have never investigated a case like this before and did not know how to proceed. I assure you I will never do anything in your jurisdiction again without first attempting to speak to you."

"Thank you, son. How can I help you?"

Sheriff Davis had a strong drawl and even his shortest words seemed to have numerous syllables.

I only addressed him as Sheriff, Sheriff Davis or sir. I attempted to be very respectful in my words and my tone. I outlined why I came to St. Augustine and what I needed to ascertain for the widow and her family.

"Well, son, it is pretty much an open and shut case. The nigra was in isolation and was very despondent. Sometime during the night he took off his undershirt and put it through the criss-cross cell divider and hung himself."

Sheriff Davis was very matter of fact; nothing complicated in his view.

"Would you mind, Sheriff, if I asked you a few questions for my edification, sir?"

"Shoot away, son."

"Did you know the deceased, sir?"

"I knew of him. But I had no personal contact."

"What did you know about him, sir?"

"He was in a lot of these damn demonstrations. Making trouble. Disturbing the peace."

"Was that why he was arrested?"

"Basically, yes"

"Did he make any calls after he was arrested?"

"Not that I know of."

"Sheriff, what leads you to believe that he killed himself?"

"Well, son, it is not just me, ya know. There was a grand jury investigation and they concluded that it was a suicide."

There was a certain smugness in his voice as he said that. As if to say don't bother---the case is closed.

"Oh, really?" I paused in surprise. "How many days after the death did the grand jury investigate?"

"Two, maybe three."

"Did they deliberate for a few days?" I asked naively.

"No. Took maybe an hour. Not much to analyze really."

"What evidence was presented? What did they base their decision on?"

"Well, son, he was put in an isolation cell as he was very belligerent. He was given some water and some food. As it was late, he was left by himself. In the morning when the officer went to give him some food he was hanging in his cell. The officers on night duty and the officer that found him testified to those facts. Really, not much else about the case."

The sheriff looked down at his desk while he described the scene and used a tone that indicated he did not think it was worth his time to discuss these details.

In our conversation, Sheriff Davis emphasized to me that St. Augustine was a very peaceful town and most of his cases were of minor infractions, such as public drunkenness and petty robbery. That is, with the exception of the demonstrations of the "nigras," which he attributed to the leadership of outside groups who were communist-led and were intent on overthrowing the powers that be.

He added that his police force tried to be impartial and simply enforce the law but that sometimes, in the face of "belligerent nigras," they used force that some people thought to be excessive.

"Well, sir," I asked. "If there was this racial tension, wasn't there a possibility that someone in the jail, at night, might have used excessive force, as you describe it, against the inmate, who you described as belligerent, which contributed in some way to his death?"

The sheriff stared at me intently. I could see his jaw tensing on the side of his face. "Son," he began, "I don't take kindly to any such implication for which there is no evidence. We are having a respectful conversation here. Let's try to keep it that way."

"I am greatly appreciative of you taking time to speak with me about this case and I am not implying any misdeeds on the part of your officers. However, given your own words about the local situation here between your officers and the Negro population, wouldn't it be wise to verify that no one reacted to the deceased's belligerency? What evidence did the grand jury examine to come to the conclusion that the deceased hung himself?" I added.

"The county attorney called officers who were on duty from the time he was arrested until his body was discovered. He cross-examined them. Pictures of the deceased were also introduced into evidence. Then a conclusion was arrived at. This is all part of the public record."

I thought for a moment and then asked what I thought was a crucial question. "Could I see those pictures, sir?"

To my surprise, the sheriff rose up. "Of course you can see them, son."

He went to his file cabinet and removed a thick file. There were numerous black and white photos, 12 to 15. He put them all in front of me on top of his desk. "Have a look."

I took the pile of black-and-white glossy photos and began to examine them in silence. They were about 5" x 8" and very clear. All of the pictures were of the deceased lying on the floor of his cell. None were of him hanging by his shirt. I thought that was shocking. Why have so many pictures of him lying on the floor from different angles and not have one of him hanging?

Innocently, I asked him, "Sheriff, was there a chair in the solitary confinement cell?"

"No" he replied. "A chair could be used as a weapon."

"Is there a coroner's report?"

"No, there is not."

"Have you seen many hangings, Sheriff?"

"Not really, son. Hangings are not common any longer here."

"Sheriff, would you allow me to inspect the cell where he died?"

"Sure, son. When would you like to visit?"

"If possible ... now"

"I will call the county jail now. Go ahead."

"Can I come back here afterwards, in an hour or so to discuss this situation?"

"Of course, son. I will be here the rest of the afternoon."

"Thank you, Sheriff."

We shook hands and I left. I returned to the jail just outside of town. I was a little apprehensive, not wanting to revisit that dog. When I arrived the officer was almost welcoming.

He took me to the cell. The walls were smooth cement. No irregularities to use to rise off the floor. The door was made of steel connecting to two steel dividers that were joined to the cement walls.

The top part of the walls had small criss-cross openings, also made of soldered steel. The openings were there to allow air to come into the cell. They were less than an inch wide.

My fingers could not go all the way through them and I was very thin at that point in my life. Additionally, they were above my head and I was 6 feet tall. The deceased was listed at 5 feet, 6 inches tall.

I had a Kodak camera and took pictures of the cell at all angles. Clearly, with nothing to raise him up, the deceased could not have hung himself. Furthermore, the holes were too small for him to have slipped his shirt through and returned the shirt back through another hole, even if he had a way to raise himself up. It was clear that he did not commit suicide in this cell.

I looked at the officer on duty with my best poker face. I just stared into his eyes. He looked away. I just stood there letting my conclusions sink into my head, deciding what to do next.

He spoke. "Anything else?"

"Officer, were you on duty when the deceased entered the jail or when he was found hanging?"

"The sheriff said I should not discuss this case at all. He would answer any questions you have."

I did not bother to try to get him to talk further and motioned that we could leave. Fortunately the dogs were separated from the area I was in and I peacefully left the jail and returned to Sheriff Davis' office.

(In today's St. Augustine, the jail is much bigger and there is a separate wing to house an expanded version of the sheriff's office. The isolation cell is still there, according to Jimmy Jackson but when I returned there in September 2018, I was denied entry as the cell and the jail were occupied.

Chuck Mulligan, the press attache in 2019, says the isolation cell in question no longer exists. Outside the sheriff's office there is a bronze statue of a German shepherd with a thankful dedication for reliable service).

The sheriff smiled as he led me into his office once again. He acted as if we were two old friends reuniting. I sat down at the opposite end of his government-issued desk, searching for the right words to reopen our dialogue. He waited for me to speak.

"Sheriff, I do not have a lot of experience in these types of cases. You have had maybe thousands of cases. I am sure this is old hat for you. That said, Sheriff, there is one thing we both know for sure."

He looked at me quizzically. "What would that be, son?"

I paused to carefully choose my words.

"Sir, please don't take this personally. You are clearly a smart man. You have a long career in law enforcement."

"Yes, son?"

"Sir, we both know for sure that this man did not commit suicide."

I looked at him with a blank stare, awaiting his reaction.

He looked at me, his mouth open more than usual. He hesitated. He clearly was not expecting me to say that and his surprise became obvious as the seconds of silence elapsed. Finally, he spoke. "Son, this is a closed case. The grand jury has spoken. Everything that had to be done has been done. It is not for me to wonder why."

"Well, Sheriff, that may be the case but it is clear to me that the grand jury rubber-stamped the evidence it was given without the slightest attempt to verify the facts of this case. The most rudimentary investigation would leave it clear that a crime has been committed here and that the very people that testified as to how the deceased died were not being truthful," I told him.

But then I added, "I appreciate your openness in allowing me to see the evidence and the jail cell. If you allow me, I will return to say good-bye before I leave early next week. I hope that while I am here I can count on the equal protection of the law from your office."

"You are welcome son. Surely you will be protected here. You are very professional and very respectful. I wish everyone that wants to change our way of life would have the same approach that you have. I hope to see you again under the same circumstances."

We shook hands and I left to go to Mrs. Plummer's house. I was unsure if the sheriff would in fact ensure legal protection. He was smooth and had the southern manner, as it were.

But that did not suppress the clear fact that he could not care less that the deceased black man was deprived of any civil rights under his watch. The legal formalities were followed but the substance of the law was totally ignored. Under his watch a man was murdered in his jail, the county jail of St. Johns County, and he simply ignored this horrific fact. Additionally, he was complicit in its cover-up.

I related what I found to Mrs. Plummer. I could not hold back my shock. She nodded as I described all the reasons why there was no conceivable way this was a suicide.

"Welcome to St. Augustine," she said dryly. "This is what we live with here on a daily basis. There is simply no respect for the rights of Negroes in this town."

She suggested I take her car over to the local hangout and get something to eat and maybe meet some people my age to let off steam. I thanked her and decided to follow her directions to Harlem Gardens.

As I drove off, the road took me out of town and onto a dirt road. It was full of ruts and I had to drive very carefully and slowly. Seemingly out of nowhere, a police car started following me. After some five minutes, the flashing lights began and I stopped the car. The officer approached and I rolled down the window. He asked for my driver's license and I gave it to him.

"Where you goin' boy?"

"I am heading to a place called Harlem Gardens, officer"

"Ya know that's a nigger hangout, boy?"

"Actually I was only told it was a place I could get a hamburger and a Coke and listen to some music, officer."

"Get out of the car!"

I did as I was told. We were about the same height---6 feet. I guessed he was a few years older than me. We were both white but once again, that's where the similarities ended.

"Ya driving a nigger car, boy. Where did you get it?"

"Mrs. Plummer lent it to me, officer."

"So I gather you're not from around here, boy."

"No, sir."

"From up north, I see."

"Yessir"

He took his gun out of his holster. "We don't take kindly to outside agitators here in our town."

"Well, sir, I just spent some two hours with Sheriff Davis, officer. We discussed the details of why I am here and he indicated he was fine with that."

He placed the gun on my cheek. It was cold. I stared at him, straight in his eyes. I did not flinch. I have no idea now where I got the courage and I had no idea then either. He pushed hard against my cheek and I pushed back so as not to bend in any way.

He slowly pulled the gun away from my cheek and slid it into my mouth. We stared at each other. I had no idea what was the proper protocol here so I did not move.

"I could pull this trigger and end this conversation and no one would give a fuck, boy. No one."

I continued to look at him, silently. Suddenly he pulled the gun away and holstered it.

"Get the fuck out of here! Get in your nigger car and go to your nigger bar."

By now I was having a little trouble breathing and silently, but with pace, got in the car and continued down the road. He watched me go until I was out of sight.

In my recent talk with Jimmy (Jackson), the St. Augustine civil rights activist, he assured me that the officer was Deputy Everett Haney, who he described as racist with a sadistic bent.

Regardless, it was the scariest moment I had in northern Florida in the summer of 1965. As I drove slowly down the road, my hands started to shake. My breathing became difficult and I had to make an effort to take deep breaths. I felt something coming up behind my throat. I stopped the car and got out. Within seconds I was vomiting and my whole body was shaking. Finally I regained control of myself and got back in the car.

Driving toward Harlem Gardens, the ruttiness of the road made driving a challenge. I could only imagine driving on it when the rain came down. It reminded me of the roads into Florida A&M, another glaring example of the untruthfulness of "Separate but Equal."

The place was a large indoor/outdoor venue with various bars, great music and a variety of different areas to sit. I chose a couch, after ordering a hamburger and a Coke.

I went to the men's room to wash my hands and face. There were no separate bathrooms here. This was the only public place I saw in Florida that did not separate the races in order to use a bathroom.

As it was quite early, the place was about half full. After I downed my food, a couple of black women came over with a very young white couple. They knew Mrs. Plummer and introduced themselves.

The two whites were Quakers living in St. Augustine for the summer vacation from college and had very little to say. They demonstrated apparently when called upon and worked with little kids most of the time. The two black ladies, who were a few years older than me, were very outgoing and discussed in detail the situation in which they lived. The racism was exhausting, they volunteered, and they intended to move away in the near future.

We were joined by more people, most of whom were curious to learn who the new white boy was. As time passed the place began to fill up. After a while, a young, wiry black man came into the group, learned why I was there and asked me, almost challenging me, if I would go with a group to the "white" beach tomorrow morning.

I said I might, depending on what plans Mrs. Plummer had for me. He said he would speak to her and that we would go about 9:30 the next morning if she agreed. I said that worked for me.

The man advised me quite clearly that he did not believe in non-violence and would respond accordingly if hit by anyone. I told him I was with Sheriff Davis for a good while this afternoon and would like to advise him of our plans. He vetoed that idea violently.

"The sheriff is our enemy. Don't be confused. He won't help us. He will set us up for something bad. We will go and see what happens."

"Look, I have no experience here except for what I saw today. You live here. I will do it your way," I told him.

And that is how it was left. After a while, I said my good-byes and made my way back to Mrs. Plummer's house. We talked for a while and she told me we would all go to the beach tomorrow.

The next morning, after a nice breakfast of bacon and eggs prepared by

Mrs. Plummer, she drove us to a location within Lincolnville where some six cars awaited her arrival so as to head off to the beach.

After a 15-minute drive heading out of town and over a bridge spanning the Intracoastal Waterway, we turned onto a simple road that led us to a rather large beach. In St. Augustine, the sand is quite packed down with room for a multitude of cars to park not far from the water. In the area where we stopped, there were already some seven cars and people, all white, were ahead, near the water.

Our cars emptied and everyone headed to the water. To my surprise, there were about 15 children piling out of the cars, accompanied by the two Quakers from last night and three black women.

The only other man, besides myself, was the young, black wiry man from last night who organized the event. I had never been part of any type of demonstration in Florida before where the group did not have a large majority of men.

As the kids played in the shallow surf, I noticed that very few were actually swimming, probably because they never had access to pools or swimming lessons, not to mention that they were very young.

I had a very eerie feeling about this adventure. I walked down to the water's edge to make sure the kids were okay. As I turned around with my back to the water I saw a few pickup trucks arrive and park near our cars, about 30 yards from the water. The kids would be totally unprotected if there would be a confrontation.

A number of older white men got out of the vehicles. Unlike our group, they were not wearing beach clothes. As I walked away from the water, more and more pickup trucks arrived with similar-looking white men. As I got closer, I noticed a few with bats in their hands. Almost all of the trucks had some type of Confederate flag displayed: a license plate, an actual flag or different types of stickers.

Within some 15 very long minutes, a group of at least 30 vehicles had gathered, almost all of which were pickup trucks. Most had rifles in their back window. Virtually all of the occupants were white men, much older than me, perhaps in their 30s and 40s. I could not imagine an uglier scene.

Soon the lone black man was in a fist fight with a much bigger white man. The white man went down with a couple of rapid punches. I approached Mrs. Plummer.

"How does this look to you, ma'am?"

"Not too good."

"Don't you think it is time to call the sheriff?" I asked.

"Yes, I do."

I looked at her. "Where would I find the nearest phone?"

"There is a grill down thataway," she said as she pointed down the beach. "There should be one there."

I started running off down the beach. I could not see any buildings, but I kept running in the direction Mrs. Plummer had pointed to.

I heard some voices behind me and as I turned to look, I saw three portly men running after me. I was in very good shape and they weren't. I did not think they would catch me but their chasing me gave me extra motivation for going fast. After about 15 minutes, I saw, behind what looked like a dune, a round, rather large building which I guessed would be the beach grill. There was smoke coming out of an area on the roof, perhaps from food on a grill.

The odd-looking building was totally round outside and inside. There was one entrance/exit and as I entered, I looked around for a cashier or someone who looked like a boss. Across the room, at the opposite end of the large room's circumference was a tall, older man preparing some food. I ran up to him and told him there was an emergency on the beach and could I use his telephone for a quick call.

"Sorry, son, we don't have a phone here."

"How can I make a call, sir?"

He pointed down the beach. "There are a number of houses nearby and I am sure one will let you use their phone."

I nodded, thanked him, and turned to exit where I entered the grill. However, waiting for me at the entrance were the three rather portly fellows breathing heavily, the ones who were after me. I gingerly approached the large doorway that they were partially blocking.

My mind was racing, looking for a way to pass them. Suddenly I ran at the right corner of the exit and they all lunged as one in that direction. I stopped on a dime and sprinted out the left side space before they could adjust their positions and reach for me. I ran down the beach, away from the grill and quickly saw a house.

Within five minutes, I arrived there and knocked on the door. A man opened it and I told him I had an emergency and would he be kind enough to allow me to use his phone for a short, local call. He agreed and waved me in, closing the door behind me. He pointed to a phone in the living room where his family was gathered.

I dialed 0 and an operator picked up. "Could you please transfer me to the sheriff's office. It is urgent," I said.

Surprisingly, the sheriff himself answered immediately. "Sheriff Davis, this is Frank Reider. We spoke for a while yesterday."

"Yes, son, how can I be of service?"

"A group of Negroes came to the beach to swim and there are some 30 people who arrived shortly thereafter to prevent them from so doing. I think the risk of violence is very great. I must emphasize that the group is almost all children and women."

"I will take care of this right away."

He hung up.

The homeowner was not pleased. "You sonuvabitch," he shouted. "Get out of my house!"

"Yessir," I replied as I looked at his disapproving family.

I noticed a very attractive girl sitting there, staring at me open mouthed. I smiled at her before I asked her father, "Would you perhaps have a back door I could use to leave you alone?"

"Goddamn right I do. Right over there," he said pointing in the opposite direction from where I entered.

"Thank you, sir," I answered. "You did the right thing."

I smiled again at his daughter and ran out the back door, down to the beach and headed back to where this all started. I saw the three men waiting outside the front door.

Almost immediately I heard the sirens from the police cars and could see their lights flashing a few miles away. I took a big sigh of relief and continued back to our rendezvous. The whole scene flashed back in my mind and I shivered in fear as to what had just passed. If it were not so serious it would have been comical in so many ways.

In my mind, the three guys that were after me became The Three Stooges. As I started trotting back to the site I had left about a half hour ago, I looked behind me and saw the three men walking slowly. Clearly they had given what they had to give. They were mercifully done!

When I arrived back at the location of the wade-in, there were over a hundred people gathered. The police apparently had taken control of the situation. There were two police cars at the water's edge and a few more near where we had parked. The police had established a human wall separating the blacks from the whites. The two police cars were on the "black side."

As I approached, I saw that the man who was the leader of our group was in the back seat of one of the police cars sitting next to the male Quaker student. Both were handcuffed. I ran up to the officer next to the car.

"Why are they handcuffed, officer?"

"Who the fuck are you?" he responded, not very kindly.

I was taken aback by the question. I began to answer but I was stuttering. *"Who the fuck was I?"* I asked myself.

"Officer, I am helping these people with legal advice," I answered, not very convincingly, however.

"Yeah, you are the nigger lover that was with Sheriff Davis yesterday!" he shouted at me. "From New Yawk, right?"

"Officer," I responded slowly and in a very low voice. "I accompanied this group of children to the beach where they wanted to enjoy the waters of St. Augustine on this beautiful, but hot, morning. No one in the group was disturbing the peace. When a group of gentlemen came here upset with the presence of the Negroes, in order to avoid violence, I ran to call the sheriff."

The officer looked at me quizzically, seemingly puzzled by my suddenly formal manner of speaking. I was not sure how much he heard nor how much he understood.

"The sheriff had already told me that he acknowledged the right of these people to use the beach in a peaceful manner. Now officer, I recognize this may not be pleasing to many people and, in fact, may not be pleasing to you as well. However, the law allows them to use the beach and you are a deputy with the responsibility to uphold the law."

I paused and took a deep breath, adding "Now, officer, given what I have just said to you and given that these two gentlemen in your police car are handcuffed after coming to the beach for a swim, and given that the group of white gentlemen standing on the other side of this police line were here to prevent them from enjoying the beach, to use your language: What the fuck are they arrested for?"

The officer's mouth fell open. He could not find the words to respond. My mind was racing. *"What did I just do?"* I asked myself. Did I really need to say all of that?

There was a pause that probably did not last more than a few seconds but seemed like an hour. I reached into my pocket and pulled out my brownie camera. I silently walked over to the police car and motioned to the two men to raise their handcuffed hands. I took a picture of them, then turned and took a picture of the now-silent officer.

He finally spoke. "Are you guys done here?"

(In May 2019, the local historian, David Nolan, sent me a copy of the Jacksonville Star of July, 24, 1965 reporting on this incident. Although I did not hear it, apparently the deputy in question said I was "white trash or he would not have been with this group on the beach." The newspaper also reported that there were about 300 whites shouting threats and throwing bottles.)

"I would need to ask Mrs. Plummer. I work for her."

"Please do that now so we can get the fuck out of here."

Mrs. Plummer was standing not too far away and I walked up to her to see what she wanted to do.

"I think we are done here," she said quietly to me.

I walked back to the officer. "Will you let them go if we were to leave now?"

"Are you fucking joking, boy?"

"No, sir," I replied. "Under the circumstances I have just described to you, I would think it would not be appropriate for us to leave the beach with them arrested, when the only thing they did wrong was come to the beach for a swim."

"The nigger punched a white guy." he replied. "That is disturbing the peace and the aggression could even be a felony."

"Officer, it would only be a felony if he hit him unprovoked. Are you alleging that he hit someone unprovoked? Seriously?"

The officer stared at me silently. He was clearly frustrated and he was fuming. Finally he spoke.

"If you give me your word that if I let these two go, your whole group will immediately get in your damn cars and leave the beach, then I will let them go without being charged."

"I give you my word. But under one condition. You keep those white folks from doing anything aggressive against our group. Not anything. And if anyone does anything against us, you will arrest them for disturbing the peace and I will accompany you to the station to verify that they are being charged. That is part of the deal."

"Don't give me any more sass, boy." the officer replied. "I am going to uncuff them and then you get everyone out of here immediately. That's the deal. Now go."

He turned and uncuffed their hands. I walked with them to the car. The group of whites were screaming, objecting to their release, cursing, outraged but not moving beyond the police line.

We all got into our cars and we drove off. No one followed us. It was not even noon. It seemed like an eternity had just ended. We drove back to Lincolnville.

No matter how racist most of the police in St. Augustine were, they still were the only defense between our demonstrators and totally anarchy. I took a full roll of pictures on my Brownie camera and would develop them at a later date in another town. They would be interesting to view but of little consolation if the police had not kept the rowdy white crowd separate from the rest of us.

After lunch, Mrs. Plummer took me to see the deceased man's widow. She and her two young children lived in a small, clean house. The widow was obviously very sad. She listened carefully to my telling of what I found and took some consolation in my conclusion that her husband did not commit suicide.

She repeated much of what Mrs. Plummer had already told me and mentioned how much he loved his children and that he would never abandon them.

The whole scene was terribly sad and we all choked up a few times during our conversation. I was angry about this whole story and could not fathom how a law enforcement officer could so clearly and irresponsibly abandon his sworn duty to enforce the law. We consoled each other and then departed.

With that in mind, I returned that night to Harlem Gardens for what had now become my everyday meal, hamburgers, fries and a Coke. At this point in my life, I did not drink alcohol nor use any drugs so I could not find any solace from these alternatives. When I sat down on the same sofa as the previous night, I was joined by a few people who had heard word of that morning's activities.

After a bit, the wiry leader of the demonstration arrived and gave me a hug. "That was some morning we had out there," he laughed. "You ready to go back tomorrow morning?"

"You are not serious!"

"Goddamn right I am. This is St. Augustine. We have to keep pounding. You with us?"

I thought about it and looked him up and down. I still had not calmed down from the day's events. I was not anxious to repeat the scene. On the other hand, I did not want to back down either.

"I will go with you under one condition. You let me advise Sheriff Davis that we are going. He has to protect us. There is no way they will let me run down that beach like I did today. We need the police there, no matter how racist they may be."

He looked at me quietly. After a while he said OK. So we agreed that I would call the sheriff in the morning before we left for the beach.

The Quaker students were there and I tried to engage them in some conversation. Initially they were monosyllabic. Then they went totally silent. They would be there tomorrow as well.

Somewhere along the evening, I was joined by a very attractive lady who told me she was a nurse. I asked her if she was in our group this morning and she said she would never demonstrate in St. Augustine. She had seen too much violence and no change at all. She saw no point in taking the risk when nothing was changing

Slowly, the place became packed and the music got louder and everyone seemed to be dancing. The two Quakers and I were the only white people in this large outdoor area. I did not go inside but I assumed there were not any others in there.

Despite that, I felt very comfortable there and I did not notice anyone who seemed to think it was not appropriate for me to be there. The nurse and I danced to some slow music and I left.

The next morning I used Mrs. Plummer's phone to call Sheriff Davis. It was Sunday and I was hit with the idea that he might be taking a day off but he came to the phone and seemed to appreciate that I advised him of what was about to happen on the beach.

After a quiet breakfast, we got in her car and joined the others for the motorcade to the beach. There were a few more cars in our group than there had been the previous day. However, I was to find out that the additional numbers were women and more kids. Once again, the only men were the Quaker, the wiry leader and myself. I brought a legal pad with me to note the license plates of the cars on the beach.

When we arrived there must have been at least 50 pickups waiting for us plus about eight deputies from the county police. The sheriff was not there but his men were out in force.

As we pulled up the crowd went insane. There was screaming, cursing and multiple threats. A deputy came up to our car and told me not to get out. This was while everyone in our cars was running down to the water.

It turned out the deputy who warned me to stay in the car was the person in charge. He told me that the crowd thought I was the organizer and an outside agitator. He said there were just too many people for him to guarantee my safety.

I started writing down license plates and taking pictures with a new role of film. Initially, the crowd stayed separate, satisfying themselves with shouting and waving various types of weapons, the most common being baseball bats.

After about ten minutes without any violence and the kids playing in the soft surf, the natives became restless. About 20 or so came over to my car and started banging on the windows, shouting threats and challenging me to get out of the car. It was pretty frightening. Then the deputy came over and told them to back off. He motioned to me to open my car door window, which I did.

"Look son, I have been here for a lot of these demonstrations. Usually the niggers have a lot more men. Today, that is not the case and I don't think I can restrain these folks much longer. Don't you think this has gone on long enough?"

"I am not the one to decide that. Please speak to Mrs. Plummer. I will do whatever she says. All I am is the person giving legal support. I do not make any decisions."

He looked at me in disbelief and grudgingly walked away to speak to her. As he did, the gang of whites came back to my car, but this time started shaking it from side to side.

I saw the deputy speaking to Mrs. Plummer and pointing at us. She shook her head in agreement and called for everyone to get in their cars. The deputy and a couple of other policemen came back to the car and the gang withdrew to their corners. She got into the driver's seat and we began the trek back to her house. Other than shouts and verbal threats, there were no further incidents as we rode away.

She was calm, almost stoic. "This is how it is here. Sometimes the violence gets out of hand and our people get hurt. It may be shocking to you but I have been through this so many times, it starts to get old. Nothing seems to change; they don't give an inch."

Later in the afternoon we met with Dr. Hayling and some other leaders to discuss the "suicide." I gave him a rundown of what I had observed and why any suicide was impossible to have occurred. In sum, I added, this gentleman was murdered either by the police or, at the very least, with their acquiescence.

Dr. Hayling was visibly upset. It was one thing to believe the worst. It was another if the facts of the case proved the worst.

They suggested to me that I should go with John Due and speak with Judge Bryan Simpson about the case. Sadly, this type of abuse of the black population, in various different forms, was part of the daily life in St. Augustine.

For me it was shocking. How could a man be killed in a jail and have a cover-up of the killing be approved by the sheriff, a grand jury of local citizens, the newspapers and, effectively, the entire population of the town? Furthermore, why didn't anyone ask why the coroner did not evaluate what was the cause of death?

After the meeting, I went for a walk from the Lincolnville section of town, where Mrs. Plummer lived, to the downtown area. Her house was small but many of the houses in this historic section were large, Victorian style homes.

It seemed that on one side of the main street lived black families and on the other side the residents were white. The center of the city was not far.

The center of the picturesque town was the old Slave Market. After what I had witnessed in the last few days, I thought that nothing could be more appropriate than having the central point of the town be a place where slaves were bought and sold.

Next to the market was a small plaza where people could gather and interact. It was also a place for demonstrations against segregation, where many black leaders were arrested, including Dr. King. Its design reflected the Spanish influence and the importance of community in the town's founding.

Nearby is a cathedral and the government house. Catty-cornered from the plaza was the impressively large Ponce de Leon Hotel with its gorgeous gardens and lovely Spanish architecture. I was literally blown away by the beauty of all of this and greatly saddened by how the town, with all its history and significance for our country, was unyielding in upholding its segregationist past in the face of all the changes going on around it throughout the South.

The frustration of the local black leaders with the unyielding position of the sheriff and other authorities toward desegregation was palpable. It seemed that the dedication of the authorities to maintain segregation was their highest goal, more than any thought of police responsibility to the common good, fair treatment of their fellow man or any religious beliefs they may otherwise have had.

They were willing to bring St. Augustine to its knees economically before ceding an inch to integration. The economic damage to the town was already severe, its image blackened by all the negative publicity nationwide.

The celebration of its 400th anniversary was subdued and ignored nationally due solely to the town's stance to maintain segregation unchanged. The sheriff, as the most powerful individual in the town and in the county, had made no secret where he stood: staunchly against any changes no matter the cost.

Sadly, we concluded that my work here was done and I would bring all the facts I found to Mr. Due to determine how we would proceed. I assured them we would strive to get a meeting with Judge Simpson about the murder in the isolation cell in an effort to achieve some type of reckoning.

Dr. Hayling and Mrs. Plummer assured me their fight for civil rights there would continue unabated. I expressed my admiration for them both. As I mentioned before, Mrs. Plummer had been fired as a nurse after many years at Flagler Hospital where Mayor Shelley was the chief doctor in charge. She had been warned and yet continued on. Dr. Hayling, whose dental practice had a white majority of patients, had lost most of his business. He would continue to press on with his role as local leader despite all the difficulties this brought him.

The next day I caught a Greyhound back to Tallahassee, terminating my stay in St. Augustine.

In 1966, Dr. Hayling, his dental practice in shambles, moved to Fort Lauderdale, Florida and started over. He could no longer sustain himself and his family in St Augustine. He lived in Fort Lauderdale until his death at 84 in 2015.

He did not return to St. Augustine until shortly before he died, when he was honored for his civil rights work and the importance that St. Augustine had in the effort to attain the change in the laws on a federal level in 1964.

Today his old office is a shrine to his work and a center for remembering the civil rights battle he led. There is a large park named after him on the riverfront nearby.

After the civil rights sit-ins in the restaurant of the Ponce de Leon Hotel, it closed its doors for good. The building was not kept up and plans were made to tear it down. However, a distant nephew-in law of Henry Flagler thought it would be horrific to destroy such a magnificent building and was able to secure funds to turn it into a college.

Initially, it was destined to be a training center for hospitality workers.

With time, the college grew. Today it is Flagler College, a four-year institution of learning with a vibrant student body in a still-magnificent building. Tours of this historic site are conducted twice daily.

In 1967, Mrs. Plummer moved away, as did a number of other leaders. Apparently Dr. Hayling was able to arrange employment for her in another town.

The president of Florida Memorial College was able to secure land in Miami and moved it there. This was crushing to the local black population as the college had many cultural events as well as an educated faculty that offered options for the black population socially. Nothing replaced this, leaving a vacuum that was never filled.

Little progress was made during the remainder of the 1960s and the black population suffered greatly. Finally, in 1970, Governor Claude Kirk removed Sheriff Davis from his position, while the federal government took steps to force integration through busing children to all of the schools in town.

By the mid-1970s the white population was resigned to the integration of its schools but racism continued. It was and still is an uneasy peace.

CHAPTER SIXTEEN

JUDGE BRYAN SIMPSON

About a week after my return from St. Augustine, John Due informed me that we were going to meet with Judge Bryan Simpson in his chambers in Jacksonville to discuss the situation in St. Augustine.

From the way he spoke, this was a big deal. Judge Simpson apparently was a fair judge with a willingness to take on the more controversial civil rights cases. He was known to summon Sheriff Davis to his chambers after learning about incidents of racial abuse carried out by deputies in his department.

The most notorious incident for which he reprimanded the sheriff involved deputies who were members of the Ku Klux Klan. After questioning the sheriff about his hiring practices, Judge Simpson ordered him to return to his chambers with a list of his deputies. Upon perusing the list, he noticed one extraordinary name.

"Holstead Richard Manucy!" the judge exclaimed. "Isn't he a bootlegger?"

Before the sheriff could answer, Judge Simpson went on, "He is a convicted felon in this court!"

After some give and take, Sheriff Davis was forced to admit that "Hoss" Manucy was not fit to be a deputy.

As previously discussed, Manucy was the local Klan leader and his "Ancient City Gun Club" was the de facto headquarters of the KKK in St. Augustine. His being appointed deputy was an illustration of the sheriff's collusion with the most radical of the segregationist group of St. Augustine's citizenry. Manucy and his cohorts used their firearms to threaten the black population. Numerous incidents of the throwing of grenades and firebombs into the houses of black citizens by his group had been reported to the police to no avail.

Judge Simpson had concluded his meeting with the sheriff being advised that: "as a law enforcement officer you can appreciate the danger … when you have members of the Klan and allied organizations in your organization as deputies."

The judge welcomed us into his chambers. He was a little taller than me and had a full head of white hair. He was courtly in manner. In sum, he represented what we all expect in a judge. He was right out of central casting.

He went right to the point. "How was your time in St. Augustine, son?"

I related what had happened with the sheriff and the obvious cover-up of the killing of a local black citizen in the county jail. There was some discussion of the horrendous racism that dominated St. Augustine life. The judge was sympathetic but noted he was limited in what he could do.

"Judge," I asked. "Would you entertain a lawsuit against the city and against the sheriff's office for the responsibility of the murder of this man?"

He responded that there was no case law at that time that allowed a county or municipality to be sued under such circumstances. Without such precedents he would be inclined to not accept the case.

I presented my opinion that such a suit, even if unsuccessful, would be a caution against the mayor and the sheriff in allowing Negroes to be attacked by the racist groups. The judge agreed but felt there needed to be some precedent for him to hear such a case in his court. He emphasized that any future incidents should be brought to his court and he would deal with them with great sympathy, as he was fully cognizant of the rampant discrimination in the daily life of St. Augustine.

Judges on the local, state and federal levels in the South reflected the mores of the communities they grew up in. Rarely would a judge break ground against the traditions of the community, and that included race relations. Therefore not only were blacks discriminated against in their daily lives but they had the same issues in the courtroom.

Judge Simpson was from a traditional Florida family. They came to Florida after the Civil War so there was no ties to segregation in their background. His grandfather served five terms in the state House of Representatives and two uncles were U.S. senators. They did not possess slaves, were not rich, but were very influential.

As a state judge, he was slow to support individual civil rights in many cases. He was promoted to the federal court by President Harry Truman in 1950.

His first position was in the Southern District of Florida, which encompassed Miami to south of Orlando. Later he was promoted to chief judge of the Southern District. Shortly thereafter, in 1961, he took the same position in the Middle District of Florida, which included St. Johns County, whose seat was St. Augustine.

Consistent with the views he offered in our conference, Judge Simpson did not view himself as a groundbreaker. He stuck to prior case law for guidance.

He was hardly a supporter of the civil rights movement initially. Slowly, he became part of a change as various cases, most prominently the Brown vs. Board of Education decision, led him to object to discrimination in his courtroom. One of his first major statements in this regard was the clash he had with Sheriff Davis about the sheriff's deputies who were Klansmen, and in particular, Hoss Manucy, as related above.

This and other incidents got him the animosity of the leaders of St. Augustine, in particular the sheriff and the mayor. Various accusations were made against Judge Simpson, including that of him ingratiating himself with northern leaders so he could get promoted within the federal judicial system.

Initially, he was not sympathetic to the marches taking place in St. Augustine. He seemed to support the idea that they were disturbing the peace. However, he was overruled in a case by a higher court and from then on, viewed the demonstrations as expressions of free speech, so long as they were peaceful.

The more cases that came to his court, the clearer it became to him that the basic issue was the unbridled racism promoted by the powers that be in St. Augustine. Throughout 1964, the evolution of his views became clear. By the summer he was active in punishing racism and supporting attempts to integrate the city and reduce segregation in public facilities as ordered by the Supreme Court and the new civil rights legislation.

In my conversations with Jimmy Jackson, he confirmed that Dr. Hayling and others had found a sympathetic ear in the chambers of Judge Simpson when they were confronted with outright racism by city and county officials.

As demonstrations increased, arrests for disturbing the peace and other misdemeanors filled the jails. Instead of trying to compromise somehow, the city leaders and, specifically the mayor and Sheriff Davis, took a hard line by arresting demonstrators and raising bail rates for them.

The overloading of the jails led to the creation of outdoor yards to keep the arrestees when there was no room in the jailhouse itself. In 90-degree heat, it was unconscionable to hold people in this manner.

Case after case was brought to Judge Simpson about the excessive bail and the conditions that those arrested were kept under. After in-depth cross examination, Sheriff Davis was again found to be violating the demonstrators' rights on various levels.

The friction during the summer of 1964 continued to grow and violence was inevitable. The authorities kept blaming outside agitators and communist groups for the worsening situations. They never entertained even the minimum type of concession for the civil rights-demands of the SCLC and local leaders.

After each decision in favor of freedom of expression of the demonstrators, Judge Simpson was accused of a variety of bad motives for siding against the city. The political cases were taken to the governor who attempted to side with the city officials and led to major clashes with the judge.

Finally, no longer willing to allow the governor to flaunt the law (and the judge's decisions), Judge Simpson advised the governor's team that he was about to hold the governor in contempt if he did not use the resources of the state to support the free expression of the movement. A constitutional crisis loomed on the horizon since Governor Farris Bryant had been elected as being a staunch supporter of segregation and was closely linked to St. Augustine's mayor.

Additionally, various U.S. Senate and House committees were investigating the southern states' actions in the repression of free speech in their states. Florida's Governor Bryant refused to appear before a congressional committee and he looked for a compromise to avoid appearing racist in front of national attention.

Under pressure, he sent state troopers into St. Augustine to try to maintain the peace and the crisis was averted.

In July of 1964, after the passage of the Civil Rights Act, it seemed clear that all organizations sanctioned by any government could not discriminate, much less segregate, its populace. The position of local law enforcement in St. Augustine was that the law was federal and that people wanting it to be enforced should speak with the FBI.

Various cases of discrimination by motel owners were brought to Judge Simpson's courtroom and finally he issued an order that all of the motels must accept all people equally. Furthermore, he required that the owners bring to him a list of the Negro people that stayed in the hotels and a list of those people who were turned away and the reasons for their being turned away. He gave the motel owners 30 days to fully integrate their premises.

In contrast, the Klan gathered to oppose the imposition of the new Civil Rights law and threatened violence against any motel that integrated. Once again there was no flexibility on the side of the segregationists and violence seemed the only likely result.

Judge Simpson also required the resignation of one of Sheriff Davis' deputies who had clearly aided a motel owner in keeping Negroes out. He severely reprimanded the sheriff for the activities in favor of segregation, a clear violation made by his deputy of the new law. He reminded the sheriff that this violated other orders the judge had handed down directly to him about his hiring practices that permitted clear racist action on the part of his staff.

Additionally, he ordered the motel owner and the deputy to pay the lawyers' fees in the case of their overt discrimination against the black man who was refused a room at the motel in question. Furthermore, he warned Manucy, other Klan members and members of the Ancient City Gun Club against taking action against Negroes who tried to gain access to motels and restaurants in the city.

The leaders of St. Augustine did not take Judge Simpson's rulings sitting down. The mayor convened local leaders, including another judge who was consistently overruled by Judge Simpson for allowing discrimination against local blacks, to determine how to deal with this new landscape. They opted for a movement to impeach him. They made statements that the judge was attempting to ruin the peace and tranquility that had always been present in historic St. Augustine and to radically change their way of life and their traditions.

In one statement from the group, it was alleged that the civil rights-movement was "a revolutionary aspect of our society, and that he (Simpson) had made himself a party to that revolution .... He had joined sides."

Despite all the rhetoric, the movement to impeach Judge Simpson went nowhere.

By the end of 1965, Judge Simpson aggressively dismissed all charges against the demonstrators, acting over and above the requests of SCLC's lawyers. His orders to desegregate became the law that had to be followed. He even ordered Flagler Hospital to desegregate or face the loss of federal funding that was essential to its financial stability.

Judge Simpson was cited as the one southern judge who "exceeded all others in his speed in enforcing the law and in his willingness to embark on new legal territory to protect Negro rights."

He was universally recognized as "a man for that time."

As a minor witness to the change that took place specifically in St. Augustine and generally in northern Florida and the rest of the South, I feel strongly that courageous judges like Judge Simpson were crucial to enforcing compliance with the civil rights laws on a step-by-step process.

Like him, the courts and law enforcement had to learn to be firm in eliminating racial discrimination from daily life. Initially it was form over substance, as drip by drip, motels, restaurants and public facilities accepted blacks without violence. It did not mean that local people liked it but ultimately it was good business practice. St. Augustine is still reeling and recovering for the misguided leadership of their community in resisting change to segregation.

It is hardly an example of true integration, even today. But basically the races live side by side without violence and access is granted to all without regard to race. St. Augustine is an amazing town, still with a population of around 14,000 and with a reduced black population of around 2,500.

By the latter 1960s, almost all of the civil rights leaders had moved away and progress seemed unlikely. But with time, the town became fully integrated. This would not have happened without people like Judge Bryan Simpson.

In 2003, a new United States courthouse was opened in Jacksonville, Florida, serving 12 nearby counties, including St. Johns County. This is The Bryan Simpson United States Courthouse.

Symbolically, with this honor, Judge Simpson's legal bravery and firm enforcement of the laws, despite heavy local criticism, not only from local citizens but also by governors, senators and other elected officials, has been recognized by this very rare honor of having a federal courthouse named for him almost 20 years after his death.

CHAPTER SEVENTEEN

ST. AUGUSTINE POSTSCRIPT

In April 2019, I received from the Sheriff's Department a copy of the results of an investigation into the death of a black male by the State Attorney's Office in February of 1965. The death was ruled a suicide that took place in the isolation cell in the county jail in St. Augustine. This is the same jail that I inspected during the summer of 1965.

Subsequently, with the help of Mrs. Gwendolyn Duncan, the head of ACCORD in St. Augustine, I was able to read a letter Dr. Hayling wrote to then Governor Haydon Burns, dated July 29, 1965, where Dr. Hayling, in his role as president of the local SCLC chapter, detailed a list of the "racial incidents" that occurred in St. Augustine.

He refers to the "hanging" in February but does not refer to another hanging or suicide during the same time period. Dr. Hayling and I had discussed my findings prior to his writing to Governor Burns and he was shocked as to the details of the impossibility of the death being a result of suicide as the sheriff, the State Attorney's Office and the grand jury claimed.

As all of the other details of the February suicide are identical to the one I investigated, I have concluded that the one referred to by the present sheriff's office is the same one that I discussed with Sheriff Davis.

The fascinating part of the February suicide was the reason the case came to the State Attorney's Office---which was not normal procedure---was "the failure of the Coroner's Jury in reaching a verdict ... as to the cause of death."

When a person dies by hanging, his neck is snapped and the cause of death is very clear. The implication that a coroner could not determine the cause of death is that he did not find that the cause of death was, in fact, by hanging.

The Sheriff's Office files from 1965 were not transferred to a computer and were all handwritten. The press attache for the Sheriff's Office told me that most of the files were lost and he could not find another file for a suicide in the jail in St. Augustine. He added that the only reason the file referenced above still exists is because the State Attorney's Office sent a physical file at the time to the sheriff and that file was preserved due to the importance of the source of the file.

The decision of The State Attorney's Office was to describe the "suicide" as did Sheriff Davis but rich in details that denigrated the accused: He smelled of alcohol, was rowdy, and screamed how his wife was betraying him with other men.

He supposedly tried to cut his wrists when he took a shower, thereby showing a desire to commit suicide. He was taken to Flagler Hospital, where he was treated for "superficial wounds" and taken back to jail. Later in the day a razor blade was "found" in the shower where he allegedly tried to cut his wrists.

He was placed in isolation and all his possessions that he could use to harm himself were taken away, including his belt. He was given a meal in the late afternoon.

When it was time to give him his next meal, the deceased was supposedly found hanging by his own undershirt tied through the diamond mesh over six feet above the floor.

The theory of the state attorney and, according to Sheriff Davis, of the grand jury, was that the deceased raised himself up by putting his fingers through the diamond-shaped mesh after putting the undershirt around his neck and was able, while holding himself up, to push his shirt through the tiny mesh openings and bring it around into a knot that would then support the hanging of his body, until his neck was broken.

This is patently absurd and totally impossible to do. As I related in the previous chapter, I could not fit any of my fingers in the diamond mesh and I was both six feet tall and very thin. Even if I were standing on a chair I could not have gotten an undershirt through the mesh opening, much less bring it around to tie a knot.

Additionally, to make the "suicide" theory even more implausable, the deceased in the February "suicide" was smelling strongly of alcohol, the implication of which was that he was incapacitated by his drunken state, according to all the deputies in the jail at the time who testified under oath before the state attorney.

Neither the State Attorney's Office in its written analysis, nor the grand jury, according to Sheriff Davis, called any witnesses other than the people working in the jail at the time of the "discovery" of the hanging body. Additionally, there were no pictures of the hanging body, only of the body lying on the floor. The excuse in the State Attorney's Office's decision was that the police had to take the body down in order to enter the cell.

According to the analysis, "It was determined upon sworn testimony, that the undershirt which was found to be tied in a slip knot around the neck of the deceased ... was tied in the diamond-shaped mesh weave of the door and was tied several inches above the head of ... (the deceased)."

The conclusion of the State Attorney's Office went on to say that the pictures of the deceased were taken "after the deceased was cut down and removed from the door in order that it could be opened, and prior to the body being removed from the padded cell.

"Therefore, it is the opinion of State Attorney's Office, after a complete and thorough investigation of the several witnesses, that the deceased ... met his death by his own hands while in the padded cell of the St. Johns County jail, by hanging."

I have made every attempt to analyze this document objectively and to try to find an explanation that could be reached that justice was served and the State Attorney's Office was not complicit in a cover-up and I simply cannot do it.

An investigation was made for the specific purpose of "Determining whether or not the deceased ... met his death by his own hands or by foul play," yet the only witnesses called were exactly the people who, if there was "foul play" would have participated in the "foul play" and would have a vested interest in covering up the "foul play".

Additionally, the most important expert witness to a death for the government is the coroner, who has the legal responsibility to determine the cause of death and, in this case, quite oddly could not make that determination.

Why was the coroner not called to ask why he did not carry out his legal responsibility as required by law? Why was there no other expert witness asked to examine the body? It is unheard of to make a determination of the cause of death without having someone examine the body.

Additionally, in his letter to the governor, Dr. Hayling makes reference to a Coroner's Jury where a Negro member voted against concluding the death was by suicide. He also notes that the local newspaper published the name and address of the person voting against the suicide!

This is without even getting to the other facts as to how the deceased gentleman was able to hang himself without any way to reach the location where the hang knot would be hung from, other than pulling himself up with his two hands, simultaneously passing his undershirt through and around the tiny diamond mesh and securing the same shirt in a manner that would withstand the weight of his body while holding his body up defies even the most superficial analysis.

This case is a shocking miscarriage of justice that illustrates how the racism of the 1960s pervaded all levels of southern life and most especially the offices that were there for the enforcement of "Justice."

CHAPTER EIGHTEEN

TALLAHASSEE

The capital of the state of Florida, Tallahassee, was my home base for almost three months while working for John Due. The town was totally segregated. Its major business was government and being the home of Florida State University. Slavery was an important part of the town's history, as the surrounding area was farmland and cotton was a significant product for the area.

The region was initially settled by Native Americans and Tallahassee gets its name from the Muskogean name for "old town." The Apalachee people were agrarians who settled there from Mississippi. Later, the Creek (Seminole) moved in.

Then Spain added a multitude of missions in the area with the purpose of food production for the settlement in St. Augustine.

Most of what was the beginning of Tallahassee was burnt to the ground in 1818 by General Andrew Jackson as he initiated attacks on the Native American Seminoles during what was later called The First Seminole War. My fellow intern in 1965, Ira Simmons, is writing a book about the three Seminole Wars that decimated this tribe. The government's army attacks were horrific and Jackson's leadership was needlessly aggressive, practically wiping out the entire tribe. Despite the attempts to eliminate the Seminoles in order to take control of their large swath of land, a number escaped to the Everglades and survive until today.

After Florida was ceded by Spain to the United States, the local governor needed a more central area for its capital and Tallahassee was chosen. Until then St. Augustine and Pensacola were the two principal settlements in the territory and the new capital was midway between the two.

In 1827, Ralph Waldo Emerson visited the area and described Tallahassee as "a grotesque place of land speculators and desperados." Various descriptions of the town have been given over the years but not much had changed in reference to its ethics through 1965.

Tallahassee was the only state capital east of the Mississippi River not captured by the Union forces during the Civil War. With the end of slavery, cotton plantations closed and much of the tobacco farms as well. Citrus farms, which continue until today, and cattle ranching became the principal agricultural developments.

Freedmen created an area of Tallahassee named Frenchtown and for a while owned the principal bank in the area. Interestingly, the land where Frenchtown was established had been owned by Marquis de Lafayette. It had been ceded to him by the U.S. Congress as a reward for his help in the Revolutionary War. He never saw the land but sent people to grow crops and produce silk.

This venture, after some time, failed. His people left to go to New Orleans or back to France. The Freedmen (slaves freed by the end of the Civil War) settled on the land and called it Frenchtown in Lafayette's honor. In the last quarter of the 19th century, universities were established in Tallahassee that would eventually become Florida State University (FSU) and Florida Agriculture & Mechanical University (Florida A&M).

The only aspect of life in Tallahassee that was different from most small towns was the fact that it housed the state legislature and had two universities. By the mid-1950s racial tension increased and incidents involving black students at A&M became more frequent. In May of 1956, two women students refused to give up their seats in the white section of a bus and were arrested for starting a riot, even though none of the passengers had objected. This incident grew out of control and eventually led to a bus boycott, not unlike that of Montgomery, Alabama and Rosa Parks. Interestingly, segregation on the city busses was outlawed in 1957 and later the bus station was named after a black reverend who helped negotiate the end of the boycott and the end of interstate bus segregation.

Nevertheless, segregation was very strict in Tallahassee, being called "Little Mississippi" and I had numerous incidents throughout my stay there. See the chapter on 'Separate But Equal" for a few examples.

Andrew Carnegie was rebuffed when he offered to build a non-segregated public library in the early 20th century. He built one on the campus of what is now Florida A&M and the main, and smaller, public library in Tallahassee was for whites until the 1970s.

The black population was quite significant, representing about a third of the total population, and Frenchtown became a very vibrant center for Negro business and culture. The only hotel in the region that accepted blacks, The Tookes Hotel, was central and Ray Charles and the Adderley Brothers lived there for a time. There were night clubs and jazz music, as well as stores, a pharmacy, Negro-only schools, many restaurants and a movie theatre.

Most hotels throughout Florida were whites-only, even in cities like

Miami, Fort Lauderdale, Palm Beach and Tampa. When Frank Sinatra had shows in Miami, Sammy Davis, Jr. had to stay in a Negro hotel in the 1960s.

The Orange Bowl in Miami did not accept college teams if they came from the north with Negro players. Numerous tourist beaches were also segregated all the way down the East Coast.

The Florida state legislature actually passed a law declaring the decision in Brown v. Board of Education null and void in the state. Although advocating 'Separate But Equal,' the legislature made no attempt to make black facilities, such as, for instance, Florida A&M, have even a semblance of equality!

Frenchtown, the oldest black community in Florida, despite all of its activity, had no direct links to the white neighborhoods of Tallahassee. Most of the important black musicians came to play at its clubs or at Florida A&M. In the '60s, James Baldwin famously came to A&M to read from his books and was refused rooms at the whites-only hotels.

Tallahassee, unlike St. Augustine and most northern Florida towns, made some concessions to integration in the early '60s, but while I was there, it was difficult to observe these modifications in action. Again, as I have written in the chapter on tokenism, integration was offered to a very few just to allow the city to say it was no longer segregated in some public areas.

However, just taking a walk in the street with a black person was enough to know that the city was not ready for integration. Numerous times I would drive through downtown with a mixed couple in the back seat and cars would start following me and approach in a threatening manner. Often they would roll down their windows and shout profanities and threats to me.

Mixed groups were not welcome anywhere in town. Demonstrations for civil rights were frequently met by white groups carrying bats and other weapons, sometimes acting violently and requiring police intervention; other times just acting in a threatening manner without any actual contact.

At the end of my stay in Tallahassee, I was exhausted by the segregation and the tenseness of trying to ignore it by going to areas that were for "coloreds only" and having to confront racists' objections to my presence in the "wrong" areas. I needed a break. I needed to have some fun so one Saturday night, my last one in Tallahassee, I went up to FSU to find a party. And I found one near the student center.

There was live music, beer and other food and drinks. Alone, I got my normal Coke and burger and looked around. A couple of coeds, drinking beer, came over to me and we started talking. After I finished my food, the three of us went outside to a veranda with our drinks, overlooking a beautiful green expanse.

The piped-in music was blasting. We were laughing and having a good time and things starting to get a little physical. My hands, free of the Coke, were around their waists and I was getting quite optimistic. They were happily chugging beers and the three of us were already old friends. In the midst of this revelry, one of the two blond, blue-eyed ladies asked me,

"What is a New Yorker like you doing down here in our country town?"

As a naive 22-year-old, when I felt a connection with a female, in this case two females, I tended to imagine that we must have similar values and interests. Then again, I had never socialized in the South with two gorgeous blond coeds. I answered honestly.

"I am working for a lawyer who defends Negroes in civil rights cases."

Suddenly my extended arms were clutching air. As if by magic, the two blondes evaporated before my eyes. The Rolling Stones were playing in the background as I looked around for my companions, oblivious to what really happened just now. "Satisfaction" was blasting; one of my favorite songs of the moment. "I can't get NO girl reaction!"

I will never forget that moment. I just started laughing at my situation. "No, no, no, no."

And so it went. Poof. Back to reality. I walked back to my apartment, literally empty-handed. I was laughing at the absurdity of the moment all the way home. Today, every time I hear the long, sensual guitar riff that opens the song I think of that night at FSU.

When I told my fellow intern, Ira Simmons, the story, we both laughed for a long time.

Ira put a period on the story. "You should have gone over to A&M!!"

CHAPTER NINETEEN

ST. AUGUSTINE TODAY

I have returned to St. Augustine twice recently; once in November 2018 and again in May 2019. I am overwhelmed with the amount of history contained in this small town of some 14,000 people. Like many tourist towns, there are tacky attractions such as St. Augustine's Fountain of Youth, which though famous, really hold little charm. But the historic fabric of the town is very special.

St. Augustine has been revitalized as a tourist center to celebrate the country's oldest city. There are a number of historic homes in addition to three forts built by the Spanish settlers as well as multiple other historical landmarks. The largest, and probably most interesting of the forts, the Castillo de San Marcos, built in the shape of a star and begun in 1672, was not completed until 1695 after 23 years of construction. It was built from coquina, a form of coral credited with enabling it to withstand all attacks.

At the center of town there is a small park, with its Slave Market, where so many civil rights demonstrations took place. In this area are a number of important monuments.

One, at one side of the entrance, is a recognition of the beating Andrew Young got when leading a demonstration in 1964. Another is a monument to the soldiers from St. Augustine that died in the Civil War.

Although black soldiers are mentioned, the monument is for the white soldiers who died on the side of the Confederacy. According to St. Augustine historian David Nolan, who was very helpful to me in this chapter, that mention only very recently took place in May 2019, when 'conceptualization' plaques were added.

There is a very interesting statement about the importance of history and the fact there are many issues surrounding monuments of the Confederacy but that this one does not advocate one side or the other but rather serves to remember history. It is a subject of significant debate among the local population.

St. Augustine was founded in 1565 by the Spanish, who built a government house that same year and a Catholic church. But war and raids over the years took their toll as Britain, Spain and France juggled for power in the Americas. Much of it was destroyed by the British in 1586, the wooden forts frequently burned, as was the town in 1740. The church was destroyed during British control (1763-1784) but rebuilt in the 1790s after the Spanish got it back, with revisions and additions later. Across the street from the Slave Market is the Catholic church and the government house, which was rebuilt in the 1930s on the original site to house a post office---a New Deal WPA project---that was there until 1975.

Only steps off King Street, which borders the Slave Market on one side, are three of Henry Flagler's iconic hotels, two of which he built, and one that he bought and refurbished as the Cordova, all constructed at the end of the nineteenth century. They are enormous and each should be seen while walking the entire area. They are discussed in detail in Chapter 13. All were inaugurated in 1888.

The fascinating Lincolnville section of town, which still has many beautiful Victorian homes and important civil rights landmarks, should not be missed. The building that was Dr. Hayling's dental office serves as the ACCORD Civil Rights Museum. ACCORD, which stands for The Anniversary to Commemorate the Civil Rights Demonstrations, has a civil rights tour which can be accessed online to allow people to follow it individually or can be followed via the trains that zip through the city. Alas, however, all the tours mainly still focus on white history.

The town of St. Augustine is integrated today and the population has declined somewhat. It is about 81% white, nine percent black, a little more than six percent Hispanic and about four % others. In the last 20 years or so, Lincolnville has become very desirable and real estate values have skyrocketed. As a result, many former residents of the community of black families there have sold their homes and moved elsewhere.

There is a vibrant historical society manned by knowledgeable people and open to the public. The street that was Central Avenue in the 1960s has been renamed for Martin Luther King and is still the main street of Lincolnville.

The Preserved restaurant is on the site of a home lived in by Thomas Jefferson's great-granddaughter and dates back to the 1850s. Located in Lincolnville, it is a gastronomical delight, though probably the most expensive restaurant in town. The Preserved has an eclectic menu and a fabulous wine list created by Christof Bauer and will delight all tastes and pocketbooks. The chocolate hazelnut dessert is as good as I have ever had.

There are other diverse restaurants, many of which are of very high quality. On St. George Street, a pedestrian street near the Slave Market, there is an incredible pizza joint, Pizza Time, and its sister store, Gelato Time, where the pizza, ice cream and espresso are fabulous.

Like most of the local civil rights leaders, Dr. Hayling moved away from St. Augustine in 1966 and established himself and his dental practice in Fort Lauderdale, Florida where he lived until his death in 2015.

In 2016, during the celebration of the 150th year of the founding of Lincolnville, the town named a large park The Dr. Robert B. Hayling Freedom Park. The park covers nine acres and sits on the edge of the confluence of the San Sebastian and Matanzas Rivers. It is a very peaceful site with beautiful views of both rivers. The street where Dr. Hayling lived was also changed to honor his name.

Mrs. Plummer moved from St. Augustine in 1967. Her small house at 177 Twine Street still exists and has a plaque that honors her and some of her famous houseguests. The house, where I stayed in 1965, is on the ACCORD tour and seems to be unchanged from that year despite an attempt to firebomb it.

At that time, very little had changed after all the civil rights activities, and the leaders were exhausted. By 1970, Governor Claude Kirk removed Sheriff Davis from office and gradually the town began serious integration, led by the federal government's forced integration of all of the schools. Local people were also tired of all the stress of fighting integration and gradually schools and other institutions began to integrate and blacks were hired by the local government.

The three hotels owned by Henry Flagler are fascinating. The Ponce is now the home of Flagler College and is certainly worth a tour. The magnificent architecture and much of the Tiffany glass has been preserved, as have the beautiful gardens in the front of the then-hotel. The students' dining room is very similar to its original state but without the opulence that characterized it when it was a functioning hotel.

The Casa Monica is interesting for its historical value. It is the only Flagler hotel in St. Augustine that is still a functioning hotel. The Alcazar is now The Lightener Museum and houses City Hall, and an interesting historic structure. All three are next to each other only minutes from the Slave Market at the center of town.

A branch of Wells Fargo is on the site of the old Woolworth five-and-dime store. Its lunch counter, where so many sit-ins took place, has been preserved in the entranceway of the bank, with a photomural in the window depicting the civil rights history of the ancient city.

The county jail complex has been built up and the 1964 jail now houses the Youth Detention Center Annex. The people working in the sheriff's office appeared to be all white and the vibe was not dissimilar to 1965. There are black officers, however, on the county and city forces._

Andrew Young made a documentary in 2015 which pointed out that as St. Augustine went into its vaunted 450th year, it had an all-white city commission, an all-white school board and an all-white county commission, all-white fire department and until recently, had an all-white police department. According to the documentary, the only change was that there had been some black police hired, mainly due to the efforts of Reverend Ron Rawls of St. Paul AME Church. Young then added that there had been only one elected black official there in the entire 21st century.

Also on the tour is the old Excelsior School, which was the Negro school, and now houses the Lincolnville Museum and Cultural Center. It is definitely worth a visit, and for those with a real interest in the civil rights history of St. Augustine, starting here and speaking with Regina Gayle Phillips, the museum director, would be of great value.

Staying in a hotel or Airbnb in the town center allows for the easiest access to the important places in town. There are numerous bed and breakfasts as well as Airbnb options.

A special boutique hotel on the edge of Lincolnville is the Collector Inn and Garden. With 38 rooms, all with some historical value, it is quite charming and comfortable. Its occupancy is high, so reservations well in advance would be advisable.

Almost everything is in walking distance from the central Slave Market and the numerous trains and trolleys can take one to every important location as well. However, I learned to really appreciate St. Augustine by walking its streets.

Today St. Augustine is a tourist mecca and quite vibrant. With the exception of the strip malls on the outskirts of town and its desegregation, the feeling in town was similar to 1965. This was reinforced upon a visit to a restaurant frequented mostly by locals. There are no elected officials on any level who are black.

The town's city officials have refused to allocate any funds to preserve the multiple locations that were important in the civil rights movement, with the exception being the tribute to Andrew Young near the Slave Market.

In the 2018 election, the vote for governor was 72% Republican in

St. Johns County, even higher than the 70% vote re-electing Sheriff Davis in 1964.

Although very subjective in value, my conversations with local blacks indicated that a lot of the old St. Augustine is still alive. In 2018, when the Lincolnville Museum went to dedicate a plaque at a location where a black man was hung by a white mob near the end of the 19th century, the plaque had been stolen and the location disfigured.

After some investigation, the indication was that the crime was carried out by a descendant of one of the men who led the hanging over one hundred years ago.

BIOGRAPHICAL UPDATES

JOHN DUE

On May 3, 2018, John Due was inducted into Florida's Civil Rights Hall of Fame. Below is the Hall's statement of his life's accomplishments:

"John Dorsey Due, Jr., was born in Indiana but adopted Florida as his home state in 1960, when he enrolled in Florida A&M Law School. He graduated in 1963, the same year he married jail-in leader Patricia Stephens. A self-proclaimed "freedom lawyer" and longtime community activist, Mr. Due worked as an attorney in Mississippi during Freedom Summer on behalf of the Student Nonviolent Coordinating Committee to monitor violence against civil rights workers. As an attorney for the Congress of Racial Equality, he helped pioneer the tactic of moving civil rights cases to federal court to avoid biased southern state courts. He also organized sanitation workers and other unions to fight poverty. In Miami, as a member of the Dade County Community Relations Board and the Community Action Agency, and as director of the Office of Black Affairs, Mr. Due's work focused on welfare rights, quality education, immigration and community policing. He helped establish a national model for community policing in West Perrine with the NAACP and then state attorney Janet Reno. Mr. Due served as lead attorney in the long-running desegregation case against Dade County Public Schools. He also helped secure the release of 500 Haitian refugee children. Mr. Due has continued his community activism in Quincy and Tallahassee, Florida, with a focus on restorative justice and the elimination of mass prison incarceration."

IRA SIMMONS

A Florida native, Ira Simmons has a Bachelor of Science degree in Political Science from Florida A & M University (FAMU) and a JD (Jurus Doctor) from Howard University School of Law where he was an Eleanor Roosevelt Foundation Fellow. A member of the Washington, D.C. Bar, he has multiple graduate degrees, became a Producer Fellow at the American Film Institute and has served as an attorney for a variety of clients, both past and present, from a number of locations and arenas around the world. His diverse life experience includes having been a student and community voter registration organizer for C.O.R.E. (Congress of Racial Equality), president of the student NAACP at FAMU during the civil rights movement, an advance organizer for the Robert Kennedy presidential campaign, an intern for the NAACP Legal Defense and Educational Fund as well as interning with the U.S. Department of Education-Title 6 team, which sought to enforce education provisions of the 1964 Civil Rights Law. He was also a team leader for President Lyndon Johnson's Kerner Commission (National Advisory Commission on Civil Disorders) report, resulting in a New York Times best-selling book published in 1968 and popularly known as *The Kerner Report.* In addition, he served as a consultant on urban problems for the California State Assembly Ways and Means Committee. As executive director of the Oakland Lawyers Committee for Civil Rights Under the Law, he participated in a program known as the Lawyers Listening Post, a group of volunteer lawyers that provided pro bono legal services to political prisoners (George Jackson, Fleeta Drumgo and John Clutchette among others) and was a lawyer in the Berkeley Neighborhood Legal Services Program as well as an elected member of the Berkeley City Council in California.

FRANKLIN REIDER

After graduating from NYU Law School, Mr. Reider went into the Peace Corps in Brazil where he helped local fisherman form a cooperative to sell their fish in Rio de Janeiro. After two-and-a-half years, having learned Portuguese and loving Brazil, he returned to the USA. There he had his first child, ran a political campaign and passed two bar exams. Deciding against practicing law, he accepted an offer from Chase Manhattan Bank and was trained in corporate lending. He was sent to Rio de Janeiro as the assistant representative of the bank. He was shortly promoted to vice president in charge of corporate lending in both dollars and local currency for Chase's local commercial bank. There he hired the first woman corporate lending officer in a market that felt women could not function in what was considered a macho boys club. He also hired a black corporate lending officer, which was very rare in the 1970s in Brazil. Almost a decade later, he left Chase after engineering a leveraged buyout of two Holiday Inns, which he co-managed for 20 years, after changing the names and upgrading the principal hotel to five stars. In 1997, he sold the hotels and moved back to Florida where he created and managed a Brazilian churrascaria in

Delray Beach for eight years. In 2010, he authored and published, *WINES OF PASSION: THE BEST OF SOUTH AMERICA.* Mr. Reider has conducted hundreds of wine tastings and wine dinners and his wine lists have won multiple awards from *Wine Spectator* and local newspapers. He is now retired and enjoys his five children and ten grandchildren, along with his wife, Vera. He intends to write books about some of his other experiences once the present volume is published.